LIGHTHOUSE

Surviving Narcissistic Abuse

A Memoir

KIA LEE

Madison + Park
A Global Branding Agency

Written by Kia Lee

Published by Madison + Park
Brand Strategist: Rahfeal Gordon
Cover Photography by Kiersten Oteyza

ISBN 979-8-9892614-0-6 (Hardcover)
ISBN 979-8-9892614-1-3 (Softcover)

Book design by DesignForBooks.com

Published 2023
United States of America

National Domestic Violence Hotline:
800-799-7233 | SMS: Text START to 88788

Trigger Warning

This book delves into potentially distressing topics, including coercive behavior, manipulation, emotional and physical abuse, violation of personal boundaries, gaslighting, control, a decline in self-confidence, and episodes of physical violence. Engaging with these themes might be especially traumatic for individuals who have experienced or are currently facing similar situations. Your mental and emotional well-being is paramount. Please approach this content with discretion. If you find yourself feeling overwhelmed or triggered, consider reaching out to a mental health professional or a trusted individual for support. Reader discretion is strongly advised.

For me.

The circle with a dot at its center is a symbol that resonates deeply within me. Throughout the journey of my awakening, this emblem began to manifest itself in unexpected places, almost as if the universe was aligning to send me a message. To me, it represents more than just a simple shape; it embodies the essence of consciousness. The circle, in its continuous form, symbolizes the eternal nature of the universe and life itself, while the dot stands as a beacon, illuminating the core of our being and understanding. This symbol serves as a constant reminder of the interconnectedness of life and the vast expanse of our own awareness.

Dedicated to my mother, the epitome of selflessness.
Your love knows no bounds, your
sacrifices are boundless.
You have given everything, pouring
your heart and soul.
Through your unwavering support,
you've shaped who I am.
For your love and guidance, I am forever grateful.

To my sisters, the rhythm of my life.
In your laughter, I find solace and delight.
Your presence is a constant source of strength.
Together, we navigate the highs and lows of existence.
Bound by a bond that cannot be broken.

To the three pillars upon which I stand,

Without you, I am but a mere fragment.
Your love, care, and unwavering belief in me,
Have propelled me to strive for greatness.
In your embrace, I find comfort and belonging.

This dedication is a tribute to your love and devotion.
To the immeasurable impact
you've had on my journey,
With heartfelt gratitude, I honor you.
For without you three, there is no me.

To those who endure in silence,
May your pain find solace within these pages.
And may the words within ignite a flame of courage.
For you, who have known the depths of darkness,
May this book be a guiding light
towards healing and wholeness.
In the silence, your voice may have been suppressed,
But know that you are seen, heard, and understood.
Through the chapters that unfold,
may you find strength,
And know that your experiences
matter, they are valid and true.
May this book serve as a testament to resilience,
To the indomitable spirit that refuses to be broken.
May it offer comfort to your wounded soul,
And remind you that you are never alone.
In the pursuit of peace and healing,
may you find solace.
May the words on these pages be
a balm to your wounds.
For you, dear reader, I offer my deepest prayers,
That you may find the strength to
break free and emerge anew.
Hold on to hope, even in the darkest of nights,
For brighter days await you on the horizon.
May this book be a beacon that guides your way,
And may you find your peace, love, and freedom.
With compassion and understanding,
This book is for you.

A Note from the Author

This is a true story. Reality as I lived it. I am not a mental health professional, and this book is not intended as a clinical diagnosis of personality disorders. Instead, it is a personal exploration of my own experiences and observations. I hope that by sharing my story, it can provide insight, comfort, and validation to those who have gone through similar experiences.

"Narcissists only surround themselves with people who enable their behavior, ignore their behavior or encourage their behavior. Anyone who tries to hold them accountable, will be blamed and accused of the exact things the narcissist is guilty of. And those that know the truth, will remain silent."

—Jill Wise, *The Enlightened Target*

Inside I am a raging ocean.
The waves of expectation keep me
just below the surface.
I feel the faint pull at my ankles.
My body is being pushed and pulled in every direction.
The currents are strong—always changing,
pulling me further and further out.
I fight the current—only to become its slave.
At times I want to drown but I can't seem to sink.
My lungs are burning as I choke on the foam and pain.
From afar everything appears calm and
peaceful, but here the weight of the
water is bearing down on me.
I want to call out.
I grasp for anything only to have the
water slip through my fingers.
I open my eyes as the wave passes over me.
Now everything is calm.
I can struggle a little while longer.
Stuff it down.

Contents

Preface

Longing for the fundamental bond of a father's love was a relentless yearning that shadowed my existence. His persistent emotional and physical absence left an echoing void in my life, affecting my path in profound ways I could hardly grasp. This deep-seated desire for paternal affection infiltrated the very core of my identity, influencing my decisions, relationships, and overall well being. Over the years, I found myself drawn towards mirages of fulfillment, which instead led me into precarious territories. These pursuits, fueled by an unmet longing, bled into my relationships, leaving a significant imprint on my choice of partners and my perception of self-worth. Struggling in this maze of unsatisfied longing and futile pursuits, I often skirted dangerously close to an abyss of despair, the edges of which threatened to consume my very existence. This is my narrative, an honest and deeply personal account that arises from my struggles. It's an exploration of the truths and experiences that have shaped my identity. In sharing my journey, my aim is to shed light on the shadows that some of you may find eerily familiar, and to serve as a beacon for those finding their way through similar adversities. Through these pages, I extend an invitation to walk alongside me on this path of understanding, personal growth, and healing. I hope that my story reverberates with those who've faced comparable challenges and that it underscores the potency of self-love, discovery, and the indefatigable resilience of the human spirit.

PART 1

Mind-craft

Stuff it down. Don't wear your heart on your sleeve. They will use it as a weapon against you. Your kindness is a weakness that will be preyed on over and over. It's OK, let them have it, yours is coming. Don't fight. They are better. They always take. They will always choose them. Don't cry. Tears are a waste of time. You are not lovable. You are not deserving. You are not enough. You are the reason why they will never choose you.

Keeping my innermost thoughts to myself has been a long-standing practice, born out of a reluctance to burden others with my troubles. We all navigate our unique struggles, so why pile on more? *Stuff it down.* It was easier to bury everything deep within, maintaining a facade of normality. As a child, an innate sense of destiny glimmered within me, whispering tales of extraordinary achievements and grandeur, coaxing me towards the enthralling allure of New York City. Here was a place that promised an expansive stage on which I could etch my mark in the world. However, beneath this steadfast determination hid a gnawing apprehension and self-doubt. The whispers of '*You're undeserving*,' '*You're not enough*,' and '*You're scared*' were constant companions, even as I yearned to unlock the dormant truths of my being. At eighteen, stepping away from the comforting familiarity of home, I embarked on an adventure that would irrevocably shape my life. The American Musical and Dramatic Academy served as a rite of passage into adulthood, a diverse, vibrant melting pot reflecting the splendor and imperfections of humanity. Within this tapestry of varied souls, I encountered my own reflection, revealing hidden aspects of my personality. Accusations of '*You're unattractive*,' '*You don't belong*,' and '*You need to try harder*' echoed in my mind. This was the time when I grappled with my defensiveness, a self-protective armor that I habitually donned, unaware of its potential to wound those in my proximity, including myself. I couldn't understand why everything felt like a battle. I clashed with vulnerability, and the ability to lay down my defenses and embrace the authenticity of raw emotions. *Don't wear your heart on your sleeve. They will use it as a weapon against you. Stuff it down. Don't let anyone hold you back. Push.* As I delved deeper into the essence of my identity, I confronted my selfish tendencies. This was a jarring revelation, leading me to question my motives, my purpose, and my self-worth. *Who am I? Why am I doing this? Why am I here? Am I good enough? Stuff it down.* Realizing the instances when I prioritized my desires over others' needs was humbling. This understanding ignited a yearning within me to cultivate empathy, to offer compassion to myself and more importantly to those around me. In the crucible of this diverse environment, I discovered my emotional fragility. The slightest slights, the most minute gestures, could trigger a surge of hurt that threatened to engulf me. *You are not enough. You are not worthy. You look weird. You look so different. Why do they always stare? It's because you are ugly. Stuff it down.* However, I recognized the necessity of facing myself squarely, confronting my flaws, and wiping clean my metaphorical mirror. All the while, I was caught in a persistent struggle, battling an internal narrative that I hadn't realized I was caught up in. The discovery that I had been living in survival mode was shocking, but it catalyzed my journey toward self-understanding. Armed with a modicum of self-awareness and an unwavering resolve, I found myself on the brink of a transformative journey, treading the delicate line between who I had been and who I aspired to become. This is my journey, my evolution, born from the revelations and self-examinations of a younger me, eager to unburden her soul and step into her true self. At the core of my journey is the enduring axiom from Neale Donald Walsch: "Be a light unto the world, and hurt it not. Seek to build, not destroy." These words serve as my compass, my guiding star, in the broad expanse of life. This is more than a simple quote; it's a philosophy, a beacon, that illuminates my path. Providing direction in times of uncertainty. This quote became the bedrock of my evolution, instilling in me an inherent desire to contribute positively to the world around me. It urged me to be a source of inspiration and kindness, to cause no harm, and to foster growth and progress wherever possible. It implored me to build bridges, not barriers; to promote understanding, not discord; to lend a hand, not turn a blind eye. In essence, it emboldened me to illuminate the world with my light and be a force for good.

Survival of the Fittest

Survival in New York City is an accomplishment in itself. A city so formidable, it is often said, "If you can make it here, you can make it anywhere." This mantra became my driving force as I packed up my high school bedroom, squeezed my belongings into my mother's minivan alongside my two sisters, and set my sights on the city that never sleeps. The stage was set, and the stakes were high. I had dreams as vast as the cityscape: to be a Broadway star, to provide a comfortable retirement for my mother, to own a penthouse on Park Avenue. Ambitious dreams, grand plans, and immense pressure. Yet, I reassured myself, don't let the fear show. Stuff it down.

Though my talent was concealed behind a fortress of fear and self-doubt, life had a way of steering me toward my intended path—New York City. The city was a vibrant, pulsating metropolis, but also a stern tutor. It taught me the value of common sense over any book wisdom and the solace money could bring by alleviating unnecessary hardships. The pressure I imposed on myself was enormous. Success, as I defined it, was a ticking clock: marriage by 28, children by 35. *Don't settle, don't dare to retreat to Pennsylvania*—there was nothing there for me. Yet, the loneliness I felt during my first year in New York was unparalleled. I spent long hours in Bryant Park because I could only afford a couple of city trips per day. Auditioning relentlessly, competing against a sea of beautiful people. I felt like I was in competition with every single person. Fighting hard to stay in the light. Fighting hard to figure out who I was. *What is meant for me?* Simultaneously wrestling with existential questions of identity and belonging: *Where do I fit in this world? Why is everything so excruciatingly expensive?* Throughout this tumultuous period, I played the part of someone who had it all figured out, not realizing how transparent our internal worlds can be. An undercurrent of longing, a void left by my absent father, colored my interactions. This void, however, was an unconscious specter in my life, driving me to seek companionship online. I believed that having a partner would somehow fill this unnameable emptiness, subscribing to the "when I have, then I will be" frequency and seeking external validation to determine my self-worth. A pivotal event in my life forced me to take a hard look at myself. This introspection, however, was of a different magnitude. The lesson learned was not just transformative; it marked a seismic shift in my personal development. The catalyst was an encounter with an individual I met on an online dating website. On the surface, this person appeared benign, hardly hinting at the imminent turmoil. Little did I know, he would soon morph into the antagonist of my real-life horror story. My life took a turn so terrifying that it seemed to exist within the realm of nightmare rather than reality. In the wake of this traumatic experience, I undertook a profound journey of self-examination. Committed to understanding my actions and choices that led to these distressing events, I scrutinized my thoughts, behaviors, and decisions. As a firm believer in introspection, I recognized the necessity of this inward journey to comprehensively understand my role in the incident. This conscious reflection led to accountability, which in turn fueled my personal growth amidst the complexities of the aftermath. Our connection started on the platform of a popular dating site, gradually transitioning from website messaging to texting and then phone calls. At that time, I was touring, a thrilling period in my life. *Singer, Dancer, Actress—a triple threat! Proud union member living the dream! Living MY dream!* The initial excitement of this new relationship, combined with the adrenaline rush of my professional journey, made it all the more challenging to foresee the impending storm. *It was nice to have someone. Someone to check in with, share your worries, share your happy moments.* Once the tour ended I returned home to New York City and we had our first date out to dinner. Things were easy. Things were fun. *Everyone always says it will be easy. That is how you will know. This is feeling easy! Maybe this is finally it for me.* As the weeks rolled on, our time together naturally expanded, filling the months leading up to my next out-of-town engagement. It seemed almost serendipitous. However, as we grew more entwined, an unsettling shift permeated our interactions. His aura felt disconcerting, a divergence from his prior demeanor. My nights became increasingly disturbed by unnerving dreams in which he covertly rifled through my phone while I slept oblivious. Even though they were just figments of my nighttime imagination, these dreams introduced an unsettling shadow into my daylight hours.

Inexplicably, even the aroma of his kisses which were once endearing now elicited waves of nausea. It was as if my subconscious was alerting me, through senses and dreams, to an unseen menace. It was during our final evening together that a disturbing incident amplified my disquiet. A common delay on the subway, triggered by smoke on the tracks, provoked a startling overreaction in him. He lashed out, accusing me of deceit and threatening that I would face retribution. His accusations, seemingly yanked out of a cinematic drama, left me in a state of bewilderment. His words, soaked with ire and paranoia, echoed chillingly, "You'll have to pay." This unexpected tirade cast an ominous shadow on our relationship, unmasking a side of him I had never anticipated. *Pay? Pay for what? What is happening?* The subsequent days spiraled into an abyss of torment I had never before encountered. His actions reached new heights of insidious manipulation, breaching boundaries, and violating my personal space. He infringed on my privacy by hacking into my email, and seizing my personal information as a weapon of control. In a perverse effort to demean me, he created explicit content by exploiting my likeness without consent. *How is this happening?* The situation darkened further when he cunningly created a counterfeit email account, mirroring mine, and fabricated a chilling suicide note. This atrocious act, meant to sow emotional chaos, was a stark demonstration of his cold-hearted maliciousness, revealing the depths to which he was willing to sink. *What the actual fuck.* His derangement appeared to know no limits. Increasing the affliction, he duplicated my contact list, dispatching the fabricated explicit content to any male contact in my address book. My phone was inundated with relentless calls, no matter the time, each one teeming with threats and pronouncements of his calculated intent to dismantle my life piece by piece. The entire ordeal stemmed from his unfounded conviction that I had lied about a mundane subway delay due to smoke on the tracks. *All of this because of me? Or all of this because this is what he does? All of this darkness because I had let this person into my life. He seemed nice! We wanted the same things in the beginning. How could someone change so fast? What did I miss? What did I miss?* In my longing for connection, I prematurely trusted someone who would ruthlessly betray that faith. The burden of my innocence bore heavy, intensified by shame and a debilitating fear that gnawed at me. The consistent torrent of his threatening phone calls, reaching both my cell and office line—sometimes while the NYPD listened in, underscored my terror. Overwhelmed by the magnitude of the situation, I found the courage within me to confide in my parents, seeking their guidance and support amidst the madness. By then, my relationship with my father had waned to infrequent, brief conversations, restricted to a couple of times a year—if he responded to my calls at all. In contrast, my mother and I shared a strong bond, conversing daily, sometimes even multiple times. Upon hearing about my ordeal, she mobilized immediately, providing instant counsel and aid. Manifesting her unwavering affection and worry, she journeyed to New York City to stand by my side, ensuring I felt secure and cherished. After a series of frantic texts and voicemails, begging my father to contact me, he finally did. However, his response fell far short of my expectations or the support I needed at that juncture. Rather than demonstrating empathy, compassion, or understanding, he berated me for my "stupidity," placing blame on me instead of offering the assistance I was so desperate for. *How could I be so stupid? How could I be so stupid to think that you were capable of providing comfort or support?* I abruptly ended the call, severing the tenuous connection between my father and me once and for all. *How could I be so stupid? How could I be so stupid? How could I be so stupid? Stuff it down.* At the time, I was entirely oblivious to the existence of intricate software capable of penetrating my online defenses, capturing my keystrokes, and compromising the security of my email. I was equally unfamiliar with the technological prowess that enabled someone to forge calls from any number and with the swift delivery of intimidating text messages. The sheer thought that there were individuals who could willingly dedicate their time and resources toward such malicious pursuits was both baffling and horrifying to me. Suddenly, I was confronted by the chilling fact that there are people capable of orchestrating elaborate schemes aimed at manipulation, harm, and control, all while justifying their actions through a warped sense of righteousness. This startling revelation exposed me to a bleak facet of human nature, a sobering reality that stressed the critical need for caution and self-protection against those who seek to leverage and exploit others for their own twisted objectives. *I never lied to this man.* Buoyed by my mother's unflinching support and guidance, I found the courage to make a definitive stand. At first, I was inclined to just "let it go," desperate for the torment to end, eager to regain control of my life. But, ultimately, I decided to seek justice, an action that would require assistance from law enforcement. With steadfast resolve, I walked into the local police station and relayed my ordeal to a detective. The troubling details of my saga seemed to stun her. Recognizing the serious nature of my predicament, she sprang into action, marshaling resources and setting in motion legal steps designed to ensure my safety and to hold the perpetrator accountable. Her prompt action and unfaltering support became a beacon of hope amid my distressing journey. The decision to file a report and press charges marked a critical turning point for me, a reclaiming of my power, a clear declaration that I would no longer be silenced, live in fear, or endure violation. Throughout this arduous process, my mother's advocacy bolstered my strength and confidence, becoming a source of immense comfort amid the storm. The actions of my tormentor eventually overstepped legal boundaries, leading to his arrest on charges of aggravated harassment. Throughout every twist and turn, my mother was there, her reassuring presence providing me with a sense of security amidst the tumult. Her unwavering faith in truth and unyielding quest for justice served as a guiding light during my darkest hours. It was in these moments that I realized the remarkable power that resides in having someone believe in you and stand by you. My mother's love and fortitude not only emboldened me to take a stand but also instilled in me an enduring sense of resilience. Her unwavering commitment to my well-being and the pursuit of justice will forever remain a poignant memory, a constant reminder that no matter how grim the journey, there's always a ray of light and support to guide us toward healing and safety. The ensuing trauma at the tender age of twenty-two shook me to my core. Gripped by an unsettling cocktail of emotions, I found myself enveloped in a suffocating shroud of darkness. An unnerving question haunted me: had I, in some way, played a role in leading myself into danger? A troubling echo resonated in my mind: "*Of course you did.*" Engulfed in this maelstrom of introspection, I found myself wrestling with the uncomfortable realities of victim blaming. This difficult introspection necessitated confronting societal narratives and internalized beliefs suggesting that victims somehow share responsibility for the harm inflicted upon them. I began to challenge these detrimental narratives and assumptions that attempted to deflect culpability from the perpetrator and onto me. The overwhelming fear that cast a persistent shadow of unease and uncertainty pushed me to retreat inward, a conscious attempt to protect my vulnerability and emotional stability. As I grappled with guilt and navigated the labyrinth of the world around me, I discovered an intense yearning for inner tranquility and a deep sense of understanding. This transformative period led me to yoga, fueling a personal journey for solace, growth, and a deeper comprehension of myself. Through my practice, I was exposed to transformative philosophies such as non-judgment and mindfulness. Yoga postures, or asanas, transcended mere physical exercise; they became portals to self-discovery and self-acceptance. In executing each pose, I learned to approach myself and others without preconceptions or bias, enabling me to engage with the world more authentically. Yoga inculcated in me the art of being present, focusing on the here and now. Each breath and movement were lessons in cultivating mindfulness, and appreciating the beauty inherent in each moment. This enhanced awareness seeped beyond the yoga mat and into every aspect of my life. I became more attuned to my thoughts, feelings, and actions, acknowledging their ripple effects on myself and others. The practice of yoga led me to the power of intention. Every pose, every gesture, and every word I uttered became opportunities to infuse my existence with purpose and meaning. Embracing a life lived intentionally, every move, word, and decision became a conscious choice, aligning with my deepest values and aspirations. This newfound mindset cultivated a sense of compassion, not only towards myself but also towards others. Through acknowledging my own struggles, I developed a capacity to empathize more deeply with those around me. I adopted an approach of kindness and understanding, appreciating the shared human experience that binds us all. Yoga served as a wellspring of self-compassion, fostering my journey of healing and self-acceptance. Yoga transformed my worldview. It reframed life as a realm of limitless possibilities, where boundaries morphed into opportunities. The idea that growth and transformation are inherent to our human existence became a comforting embrace. Yoga opened a gateway to a new dimension of existence, fostering resilience, authenticity, and a profound connection with my inner being. It served as a beacon of tranquility amidst my personal turmoil, equipping me to navigate life's challenges and facilitating a spiritual growth that had previously been dormant. My yoga journey sparked a keen interest in self-help literature, igniting a thirst for knowledge and personal growth. The realm of self-help books held a magnetic allure, offering valuable insights into self-awareness and personal evolution. The opportunity to understand myself on a deeper level and chart a course of transformative growth became a fascinating journey. Motivated by an innate desire to evolve as an individual and to have a positive impact on the world, I pursued the quest to confront and address my perceived imperfections. I voraciously consumed these books, highlighting meaningful passages and making extensive notes as if preparing for a crucial life examination. I became devoted to my personal growth, aspiring to radiate positivity in a world where darkness can often prevail. This expedition into the realm of self-help literature unveiled profound insights about my beliefs, my behavioral patterns, and myself. I began to comprehend the potency of my thoughts and the ramifications of my choices. I gleaned a deeper understanding of my strengths, my vulnerabilities, and areas in need of nurturing. These books served as lighthouses of wisdom, steering me towards introspection, self-compassion, and personal transformation. Equipped with this newfound understanding and a commitment to personal evolution, I embarked on the inward journey necessary to instigate positive changes in my life. I integrated the teachings from the books into my daily practices, implementing mindfulness, gratitude, and self-care rituals. I nurtured my spiritual connection, exploring different philosophies and embracing practices that resonated with my soul. As I deepened my understanding of myself, I discovered the interconnectedness of all beings and the profound impact of our actions. I realized that by focusing on my own growth and cultivating inner peace, I could contribute to a more harmonious and compassionate world. It became clear that the transformation I sought was not solely for my own benefit, but also for the greater good of humanity. With each page turned, I felt a renewed sense of purpose and a burning desire to share the wisdom I had gained. I aspired to be a source of inspiration and support for others on their own journeys of self-discovery and healing. Through my own experiences, I recognized the transformative power of embracing one's authentic self and living in alignment with one's values. As I immersed myself in book after book, I felt my consciousness expanding, drawing me closer to the vastness of the universe. Embracing an earnest determination, I sought to integrate the principles and knowledge gained from these self-help texts into my daily life. I believed that the familiar "fake it till you make it" strategy, so effective in my theatrical pursuits, would similarly serve my journey of personal development. However, as time passed, I came to understand that I had unknowingly distorted the essence of the teachings I had absorbed. Instead of recognizing personal growth as a dynamic, ongoing process of learning and expansion, I reduced it to a high-speed sprint against time, shackled to a stringent checklist that demanded completion within a fixed timeframe. In my zealous pursuit of self-improvement, I lost sight of the organic, complex nature of growth, reducing it to a sequence of tasks to be methodically ticked off. This approach neglected the true essence of intentional living, overlooking the fundamental truth that life is not a mere checklist, especially when our ambitions aspire to extraordinary heights. I realized that self-development is a unique, ever-evolving journey. It encompasses the acceptance of our flaws, the lessons we glean from our mistakes, and a continuous evolution of our being, propelled by a forward and upward momentum. I discovered that life's most profound lessons cannot be confined to the parameters of a list or a guidebook. Rather, they reveal themselves in the chaotic, unpredictable, and often vulnerable moments we encounter along our path. In these instances, our true strengths and vulnerabilities surface, our resilience becomes evident, and we navigate the complex mosaic of the human experience with humility and authenticity. When we open ourselves to the unpredictability and intricacies of life, we unlock extraordinary possibilities and outcomes. It is within these moments of uncertainty that we encounter the greatest potential for growth and transformation. Throughout this journey, I experienced flashes of clarity and insight, moments when my authenticity radiated brightly. Conversely, I also found instances where the mantra "fake it till you make it" was my guiding principle. Recognizing these varying experiences underscored the complexity and authenticity of my journey, reinforcing that personal growth is an intricate, continuous process, not a simple linear progression. *White knuckling my way through trauma with a smile—what could go wrong? Eventually, I will just get over my "daddy" issues, right? I am good. I am good because I say "I am good".* Regardless of the unfolding circumstances, I've nurtured the capacity to account for my actions and decisions, embracing both my triumphs and my missteps. Instead of dodging accountability or seeking reasons beyond myself, I commit to self-reflection, posing introspective questions that encourage personal growth and pave the way forward. The philosophy of extreme ownership has become a cornerstone of my thought process, provoking me to take comprehensive responsibility for my life and its trajectory. I approach every scenario with the recognition that I am the helmsman of my own vessel, and it is incumbent upon me to navigate it along the right course. This mindset imbues in me a profound impulse to scrutinize my own involvement in any circumstance before shifting focus to external factors. By embracing responsibility for my decisions and actions, I equip myself with a valuable ability to learn from my experiences and adapt, ensuring the avoidance of repeating past mistakes. The concept of extreme ownership motivates me to critically evaluate my choices, behavior, and responses. I actively search for opportunities to personally and professionally evolve, consistently aspiring to actualize my potential. This heightened self-awareness empowers me to traverse life's journey with clear direction and purpose. It fosters an atmosphere of deliberate growth, urging me to commit to a continuous cycle of development and betterment. This methodology does not just enable me to cope with life's trials but also turn them into a crucible for self-improvement. Why, then, do I persist in a cycle that does not serve me? How have I come to accept the unacceptable, welcome the unjustifiable, and tolerate relationships that suppress me, dimming my light? What core beliefs tether me to mindsets that color my choices and lure me towards situations and people who reflect the subconscious perception I hold of myself? With each repetition of this cycle, my frustration mounts. I am committed to the process of growth, following all the "right" steps, yet I can't seem to reach a point where I both choose and receive differently. I find myself immersed in self-reflection, questioning not only my actions but also my sense of worth. It leads me to a relentless inquiry—what am I projecting that attracts people who cast shadows over my existence? Throughout my life until the age of twenty-two, I maintained an innocent belief that everyone was inherently honest and would invariably act in good faith. Yet, when I ventured into the world independently at eighteen, I confronted a reality starkly different from the one I had imagined. I soon discovered that my navigational tools, adept at guiding me in a world filled with light, were inadequate in a realm shrouded in shadows. I overlooked a critical element—the principle of energy exchange. Giving light does not guarantee receiving light in return. Only recently have I become sharply aware of the presence of individuals who exploit and manipulate others for their self-serving, sometimes nefariously wicked, motives. Now, with heightened awareness, I recognize these people who insidiously extract pieces of one's essence, exploiting every resource one possesses. This process leaves victims feeling drained, and their sense of self-worth eroded. These individuals' actions are driven by a selfish thirst for power and control, devoid of any regard for the emotional wreckage they inevitably cause. Following my initial encounter with such behavior, I persuaded myself that it was a one-off incident. It was challenging to accept that the world might harbor a significant number of such malevolent individuals. *You are smarter now. You are vigilant now. You won't miss the signs ever again. Stuff it down.* With accumulated wisdom and insight, I came to grasp the unsettling reality. There were indeed more of these individuals lurking beneath deceptive exteriors. To them, life was a perpetual hunt, an endless pursuit of power and control. I found myself trapped in recurring cycles, subjected to the whims of those drawn by my radiance and goodness.

Some saw my light, their eyes glinting with a covetous desire to claim it all for themselves. They aimed to drain the essence of my being, tapping into my reservoir of compassion and love until I stood depleted, a shadow of who I once was. On the other hand, some recoiled at the sight of my luminosity, for it served as a mirror, reflecting the void within their souls. They perceived me as an uncomfortable reminder of the virtues they believed were lacking within themselves. Consumed by envy and feelings of inadequacy, they aimed to extinguish my light, relentlessly trying to undermine my spirit. Caught between these conflicting forces, I found myself entrapped in their divergent desires and expectations. Some demanded that I conform to their stringent standards, intolerant of a living embodiment of virtues they deemed forever beyond their grasp. They attempted to sculpt me into a vessel to soothe their insecurities, a marionette dancing to the rhythm of their insatiable desires. They confined me within meticulously constructed boxes, releasing me only when it served their purpose. Microaggressions poured relentlessly, a calculated campaign to belittle and suppress my true self, aiming to fracture my spirit. I remember, with painful clarity, the accusations of inflexibility whenever I resisted their demands—an irony that pierced my soul. Conformity was met with approval, labeling me as adaptable, but establishing healthy boundaries cast me as difficult, selfish, and rigid. I found my own needs and desires disregarded as they demanded my unwavering deference to their whims. Each boundary I dared set was ruthlessly violated, leaving me depleted and disoriented.

Any failure to comply with their expectations invited swift and ruthless rejection. I painfully realized that, in their eyes, I was not meant to achieve greatness that surpassed theirs. *Where do I fit in this world? Where is my partner? I can't wait to meet him. You are not enough. You are not deserving. You need to earn it. Wait to be chosen.* In my romantic endeavors, a recurring pattern emerged. Men would find themselves attracted to my vibrant energy and infectious joy, enticed by the prospect of claiming it as their own. Whether driven by the thrill of conquest or sincere interest, the outcome remained disappointingly consistent. Undeniably, the constant in these circumstances was me, an active participant in each scenario. I refrain from painting myself as a victim or a naive explorer in the territory of love. Do I classify myself as a hopeless romantic, readily swept up in the fantasy of discovering my "Mr. Right"? Am I the unsuspecting woman who invests in potential rather than tangible reality? Or am I a queen of self-sabotage, unconsciously meting out punishment because, beneath the surface, I feel undeserving? *Hello, you aren't worthy. You need to be chosen, you don't get to choose. Still down and wait until your name is called. Beggars can't be choosers. Sometimes the truth hurts. Stuff it down.* All of my long-term partners were fundamentally decent people possessing admirable qualities. While far from perfect and each carrying their unique baggage, I maintained that we were worthy of a chance. I held steadfast to the belief that all individuals had the capacity and willingness to grow and realize their full potential. Personal growth was a priority for me, and I recognized my own shortcomings and emotional baggage. My objective was never to find someone devoid of baggage or life experiences. Instead, my aim was to bond with individuals who resonated with my values and aspirations, thereby laying the groundwork for significant relationships. I was evolving, learning to follow my own guidelines, and engaging only with those whose beliefs and virtues aligned with mine. My aspiration was to meet someone who would foster my growth and inspire me to reciprocate. The goal was never to undermine myself but to trust that I would attract what I genuinely felt I deserved. However, with the passage of time, it became evident that, at a subconscious level, I must have believed that I was not particularly worthy or deserving. Despite my numerous struggles, I remained resilient. This perseverance stemmed not from self-help books or motivational quotes, but rather from a survival mechanism I had cultivated which allowed me to maintain a smile despite the pain within. I sincerely held the belief that every unfolding moment was serving me and contributing to my future, and this faith propelled me forward. There were times when my fixation on the present's potential obscured the reality glaringly evident before me. In my quest to seize the present moment's opportunities, I unwittingly made decisions that jeopardized my future and personal safety. This led me to interrogate the roots of this pattern and examine how deeply ingrained it was within me.

This realization led me to ponder: *Where did all this begin? How deep are the roots of this issue? Why can't I just "will" it away?* At times, I feel akin to a fatigued gardener relentlessly yanking at weeds, only to find they are merely symptoms, not the actual problem. My moments of relief are transitory, as I eventually uncover that the root is still firmly entrenched within me. Like all answers, the key lies in the roots of my childhood narratives. These stories laid the foundation, molding my beliefs, perceptions, and responses to life's hurdles. They have significantly impacted the way I traverse life, approach relationships, pursue success, and assess my self-worth. As we explore my journey, understand that it is shaped by my unique perspective, thoughts, beliefs, and societal lenses. These elements have played a significant role in shaping my reality, and while you may not completely agree with or fully comprehend my experiences, they represent truth as I perceive it to be. I want to emphasize that I don't claim to possess all the answers nor do I claim to be an impeccable model who has everything sorted out. In fact, the more knowledge I acquire, the more I am confronted with the vast expanse of what I have yet to learn. My intention is to share my journey with stark honesty and authenticity, hoping that it might resonate and provide guidance. I aim to shatter the walls of stigma and silence that often trap individuals in abusive relationships. If my story manages to prevent even a single person from stepping onto a treacherous path, then all this will have been worthwhile.

Innocence

Our experiences shape the lens through which we view the world and ourselves, influencing our thoughts, beliefs, and behaviors. Sometimes, these experiences can be empowering, uplifting, and inspiring. Other times, they can be limiting, toxic, and destructive. As a child I spent more energy than I care to recall, justifying unreturned calls. Receiving dried-up Valentine's Day candy in June for my May birthday. *Yeah, make that make sense.* Missed playdates that were confirmed the night prior, where I was left waiting on the curb praying for a glimpse of his white pickup truck with the red stripe. Energy in making up stories to fill the void of all the unknowns. I found myself caught in a never-ending cycle, torn between my longing for a genuine connection with my father and the harsh reality of his consistent absence. The more I held onto hope and believed in the potential for a meaningful relationship, the more elusive those possibilities seemed to become. In an attempt to make sense of his perpetual absence, I would fabricate scenarios in my mind, searching for reasons that could justify his inability to be there for me. It was a deeply painful and exhausting cycle, yet I couldn't resist the compulsion to engage in this futile exercise of self-deception. *Was he trapped somewhere? Maybe he was lost? Maybe he forgot what day it was? Maybe he is stuck at work. What does he do for a living again? Where does he live? Maybe if I leave another voicemail he will call me back. Maybe I am overthinking.* I also spent energy fantasizing about what having a father must be like. *Mom would be able to stay at home and rest and of course learn how to bake like mom-mom. I would love to have fresh cake every day! We could take vacations to places with crystal clear water in the magazines!*

We could even live in a big house and I would get my own room! I could even get my very own power-wheels Barbie Jeep! I would try to be perfect, hoping he would realize that he loves me and that he just forgot about me. *I would forgive him because we all forget sometimes.* I would call daily and leave voice messages—*daily. As an adult, I wonder how someone could listen to their child's voicemails and just not care. Can you imagine? Pressing 'play,' then 'delete,' and moving on with your life unfazed?* I needed to find a way to make sense of his absence, to find some sort of comfort in the chaos he had created. But the truth was, there was no comfort to be found. It was a lesson I would revisit time and time again throughout my life. I found myself accepting his shit behavior and secretly choking while digesting it all with a smile. *Stuff it down. Big girls don't cry. Stuff it down. Stuff it down. Surprise*—My father never came to any realization that he loved or missed me, but my ability to justify and tolerate dysfunctional behavior was on another level. This was going to serve me incredibly well. *In case you missed the sarcasm in the last sentence—oh it would serve me incredibly—but not well.* I remember running around the Grant Monument statue at Belmont Plateau in Fairmount Park, Philadelphia with my mother. I had to be maybe 3. This memory has always stuck with me. I remember running and catching a glimpse of my mother's back. I felt panic and then sheer joy when I would catch her. There was something about the running and laughter, I felt like I was floating. The love I felt was impossible to capture in a word. It was at that moment that I truly experienced love. My mother's face was love. My mother's embrace was love. Nothing else existed. No one else existed. This moment will forever be burned into my heart and my mind. I will forever cherish it. Even as I write these words, tears fill my eyes and my chest radiates warmth. *How I wish I could have just held on to that love that I felt and like a Carebear, radiated it inward forever. I needed nothing at that moment. I lacked nothing at that moment. I was completely whole. I was a Queen.* The humming of my mother's sewing machine would wake me up as the sun cascaded through the rear of our one-bedroom apartment in West Philadelphia. *Good morning sweetheart! Good morning Mommy!* It was just us. Two peas in a pod. Then, a man started visiting occasionally. Unlike the bond I felt with my mother, I perceived him merely as a courteous visitor. It's unclear when I started identifying him as my "father," or even what that title truly meant to me. I was aware of how other fathers behaved, and of the roles they played in their children's lives, and it seemed our relationship was different. *No father-daughter dances. No seeing me off on my dates. No chaperoning on field trips. No picking me up from school when I wasn't feeling well.* As I grew older, he began to visit me at my grandparents' house while I was there during the day, while my mother was at work. I could barely contain my excitement at his arrival, though, even then, I noticed a look I can now identify as disdain on my grandmother's face. His presence in my life was always transient, never lingering for more than a fleeting moment. Our interactions remained on a surface level, barely penetrating the depths of a true connection. During these ephemeral visits, he would bestow upon me tokens of affection, such as the dried-out Valentine's Day candy he gave me in June. I realize I've mentioned this before, but it's a detail that has persisted in my memory. *It's the thought that counts, right?* His assurances of attending future events were empty, along with missed birthdays, dinners, and every other significant occasion. These gestures lacked real substance, genuine love, or any meaningful impact. As I matured, I came to understand that the promises he made were just hollow words, carefully constructed to provide momentary appeasement and to conceal the profound void that loomed between us. *Why does everyone else speak their words and actions align? Who was he? Where does he go? Why isn't he around like my mother or my grandparents? Why did he only come for short visits? Did he know my favorite color? When would I see him again? How could I reach him? Does he have a family? Am I his family? Why does he always leave? Could I make him stay?* He was an ephemeral presence. Since the day of my birth, he'd flit in and out of my life with no explanation or guaranteed return. I learned not to anticipate him, but occasionally, I'd glance up, and he'd be there—only to disappear moments later without a goodbye. The memory of my fourth birthday at Chuck E Cheese is still vivid—the games, pizza, the throng of people, the cake, and him. His presence was fleeting. I recall diverting my attention from him for what felt like a mere second, only for him to evaporate into thin air. As my mother drove home, I found myself scanning the horizon for his white pickup truck with a red stripe. A hollow sensation consumed my chest, while silence consoled me, and my thoughts protected me. *Stuff it down. You are not loveable. You are not enough. Stuff it down.*

My mother chose to transplant us from the bustling cityscape to the serene suburbs of Bucks County, Pennsylvania. This transition introduced us to a panorama of expansive green fields and a sea of predominantly white faces. I reveled in the open spaces, the crisp air, and the liberty to frolic outdoors from dawn until dusk. Either the setting sun or my mother's whistle served as our summons to return home, signifying the conclusion of our day's exhilarating adventures. We pedaled bikes, frolicked in the pool, and delighted in the fresh wonders of suburban living. The change was nothing short of remarkable. *I love it here. Everything is quiet, clean, and beautiful! We have a pool! I can ride my bike in the grass!* Yet, within the pastoral serenity, I couldn't ignore the attention we attracted from those around us. Regardless of where we went, eyes followed us. I noticed the tension in my mother's demeanor, especially in large stores, but I couldn't grasp its cause. Finally, my curiosity overpowered me, and I gathered the courage to ask her, "Mommy, why do people always stare at us?" In response, my mother gently cupped my cheeks, gazing directly into my eyes. With unshakeable assurance, she asserted, "Because we are beautiful." Her words resonated with me, but the full extent of their meaning wouldn't unveil itself until I reached my twenties. That's when I began to comprehend the real reason for the incessant stares, and I recognized the profound gift my mother had bestowed upon me with her response that day.

Pawn

Back then, time seemed to stretch endlessly. I can still remember those long summers, running and playing, my laughter echoing as I chased my friends. Yet, intertwined with those joyous moments were perplexing encounters. I didn't understand why certain friends kept their distance or why others could only meet me outside their homes, never inviting me in. One memory remains sharply etched in my mind: waiting by the worn fence of the pool in Long Meadows for my friends to reappear. As I leaned against the chain-link fence, looking at a house I was forbidden to enter, a deep weight settled in my chest. The overwhelming sensation of being unwanted, unloved, and out of place consumed me. I shut my eyes, silently wishing I could just disappear. *Why are you waiting? Go home. They aren't your friends. No, be positive, maybe they are about to come out. Smile in case they are watching. Cheese . . .* In that lonely moment, a woman noticed me, and she approached me, breaking the silence that was swallowing me whole. Her voice, filled with genuine concern, asked how long I'd been waiting. I could only manage a shrug, unable to articulate the weight of my emotions. Sensing my sadness, she offered gentle reassurance, suggesting that I head home, highlighting the unfairness of the situation. Despite the emptiness brewing within, I managed a faint smile, my gaze fixated on the ground as I dragged my bike along the path that led me back to the warm embrace of my mother's loving arms.

It was at this juncture that the pieces of my fragmented reality began to crumble. The once-resilient crown adorning the head of the queen started to dissolve, revealing the vulnerability beneath. In the wake of this pivotal moment, an influx of questions flooded my young mind, accompanied by a surge of emotions that overwhelmed my capacity for discernment. *What is wrong with me? My father doesn't love me. My friends don't always love me. Where do I belong? No one wants me. I don't belong. I don't want to be here. I don't want to be anywhere. Where am I wanted? What is wrong with me? Stuff it down.* In my attempt to make sense of the complex and overwhelming circumstances, it felt as though I was trying to solve a million-piece puzzle with nothing more than a handful of scrabble tiles. No matter how hard I tried, the pieces didn't fit together, and the puzzle remained incomprehensible. I lacked the words to express my confusion or the words needed to seek understanding from my mother. I didn't want to burden anyone with my struggles or take up any more space than I already felt unworthy of. The pain I carried within me drove me to yearn for escape, I would cry silently on my knees asking for understanding. *Dear God, why am I feeling this pain? Dear God, can you make life a little easier with more love for me, please? Dear God, can you please take away this pain?* I wanted the ever-expanding void to stop—but it just kept growing. *Stuff it down. Forget the words. Forget the actions. Swallow the hollow feeling in your chest. Tears will only make your eyes puffy and your nose stuffy. Crying is a waste of time. Don't waste your energy on disappointment. You are stronger than that. Stuff it down. Stuff it down. Stuff it down.* I find that I am always running from that hollow feeling in my chest. Paralyzed, unable to cry, because I had gotten so good at suppressing my tears. I think I am afraid that if I start, I will be unable to stop. *Tears will only make your eyes puffy. Stuff it down. Perfect. Good job. Perfect. Good girl.*

I perpetually found myself in pursuit of love and acceptance, holding onto the image painted by sitcoms and movies, where love appeared effortless and readily available. Yet, as I yearned for that idealized version of love, it became increasingly apparent that it was not meant for me. The reality I experienced was far from the scripted narratives of fictional tales. I questioned why it seemed so effortless for others while I struggled to find that connection. The disparity between my expectations and the harsh reality left me feeling disheartened, believing that perhaps love was simply not destined to be a part of my story. No matter the context—whether it be relationships, friendships, career, social media, or hobbies—it felt as though each avenue I pursued only reinforced the message I'd been suppressing: "*You are not lovable.*" This belief permeates every aspect of my life, casting a shadow on my experiences and tinting my self-perception with its melancholic hue. It resonates as a somber truth in the recesses of my mind, making it daunting to untangle myself from the shackles of self-doubt and to genuinely believe in the potential for true connection and affection. Finally revealing what I have always been stuffing down: *You are not lovable. You are not deserving. You are not worthy. You are not enough. Have these words been silently echoing in the recesses of my subconscious, taking root over the course of decades? How else could they feel so true? Are they true?* The rational part of my being knows those words are not true but there is a small part of me that feels rooted to them. That small piece tethered to the little girl wearing her paper crown who only wanted love from the one person who was incapable of giving it while growing up in a place where love and acceptance weren't always mirrored. I carried the weight of those unfulfilled desires, and they continued to shape my perception of self. Despite my longing for self-acceptance and the understanding that those beliefs were not inherently true, I found myself bound to them, searching for validation and struggling to break free from their grasp. *At what point does the little girl realize that she doesn't need anything from her father or anyone else? How many birthdays or insignificant life events must pass for her to understand that her worth is not dependent on him? How many hours of therapy or self-help books must she go through? How many incompatible relationships? When will she stop fixating on something she will never receive? When will she finally look in the mirror and know that she is enough? When will she know that she is and has always been whole?*

Regrettably, my journey inward has been long and privately difficult, spanning thirty-seven years and, it seems, counting. My father, who was absent for most of my life, has left a profound impact on me. Identifying, processing, understanding, and overcoming the effects of his behavior have been an immense challenge for me. Breaking down those emotions and assigning them has been painful. We never want to believe that someone can have such a profound impact on us. We like to believe that we can just "get over it" and soldier on. I suppose I did that well. As a result, I found myself seeking self-worth and validation from external sources, primarily in my romantic relationships. My subconscious childhood narratives had conditioned me to believe that my worth was solely dependent on others, which only further complicated my journey toward self-discovery. I grappled with the complex challenge of seeking love and understanding myself simultaneously. This internal struggle became glaringly evident as I resolved to escape the cyclic patterns. The influence of my unresolved abandonment issues and my father's narcissistic tendencies on my relationship dynamics was not something I had fully realized. While an external observer might find it simple to draw connections between childhood events and relationship behaviors, the path to self-realization is intricate and never-ending. It demands not only discernment but also the bravery and dedication to foster transformative shifts in one's perceptions, values, and actions. Identifying these patterns and tracing their roots is crucial, but the real test is in leveraging this understanding to drive deliberate actions and rise above the constraints of past conditioning. It obliges me to face my own trepidations, vulnerabilities, and the entrenched beliefs that have dictated my concepts of love and self-value.

As we journey forward, my pledge is to candidly share my experiences, shedding light on the signs I either overlooked or consciously dismissed. In revealing my story with utmost transparency, I hope to shield others from the traumatic ordeal I endured, strangled literally and beaten on the unforgiving floor.

I present my scars, past, and shame, not as a testament to agony but as a beacon leading towards healing and empowerment. It is my earnest vow to amplify awareness, spark meaningful dialogues, and shatter the stifling quiet that so often surrounds those who suffer silently. Let my words stand as a guiding light, steering others away from perilous edges and towards a future where their voices are heard, their worth is cherished, and their lives are filled with the light of resilience and renewed strength. Reflecting on my past, I recognize that some oversights sprang from innocence, while others resulted from me choosing to hold onto the dream I envisioned for myself, even in the face of glaring truths. Overlooking those signs led to profound sorrow and nearly cost me my life. It's with this understanding that I commit to presenting my narrative with raw authenticity and vulnerability.

Planting Seeds

I still remember the way he used to slide into my DMs on Facebook and Instagram, with super basic and sometimes random messages like "Pretty as ever", "Hey" and "H(ow)RU?" or just a random meme. He would consistently like every photo I shared on social media and leave brief comments on my stories, but our interactions remained shallow and fleeting. There was a familiarity between us, stemming from our shared presence at the same gym over the course of several years. However, our encounters were limited to passing each other during class changes or at gym events. My life was bustling with activity, filled with double workout sessions, my job at a new fitness tech start-up, and a vibrant social calendar that often included spontaneous trips. From time to time he would suggest that we should "grab a beer". In the midst of such a fast-paced existence, I didn't have the capacity to invest in someone who didn't align with the way I approached life, and based on his social media, we had nothing whatsoever in common. *Shallow? Perhaps. Was I wrong? At that point, I was totally fine with never knowing.* In early 2020, our paths crossed once again at a mutual friend's birthday celebration. Following the event, he reached out and suggested grabbing a beer together. *Again? He is persistent.* Against my usual instincts, I decided to accept his invitation. However, a few days before the planned meeting, something inside me made me cancel. *Best not to waste your time or his.* Little did I know that a seismic shift was about to shake the world. The arrival of the pandemic and subsequent global shutdown plunged me into a state of profound loneliness and detachment. The vibrant social life I once enjoyed suddenly vanished, leaving me confined to the solitude of my one-bedroom apartment in Astoria, Queens.

The once bustling world around me transformed into a desolate landscape, amplifying my sense of disconnection from the outside world. And beyond the confines of my apartment, the world appeared to be engulfed in a turbulent storm of hate, fear, and polarization. Everywhere I turned, there were echoes of division and discord, as people became entrenched in their beliefs, drawing lines in the sand and erecting walls of animosity. The air was heavy with tension, and the once-shared spaces seemed to crackle with hate, further deepening the sense of disunity. It was a time when compassion and understanding were desperately needed, but it felt as though they were overshadowed by the darkness of intolerance and mistrust. Like countless others, I sought solace in the virtual realm of social media, a place where I could attempt to bridge the physical distance and maintain a semblance of connection with the outside world. Through the click of a button, I could share my thoughts, pour out my emotions, and seek comfort in the digital embrace of friends and acquaintances. It became a lifeline, a way to combat the growing sense of isolation and find a sense of belonging amidst the chaos. But even in this virtual sanctuary, the world of social media was not immune to the overwhelming negativity and divisiveness that plagued the physical realm. It too became a breeding ground for arguments, echo chambers of conflicting ideologies, and a constant barrage of information that left me informed, misinformed, disinformed, and overwhelmed. Amidst the vast sea of virtual interactions, his presence became increasingly prominent in my online realm. He seemed to be there, constantly observing, engaging with my posts, and leaving thoughtful comments. It was as if he had taken a genuine interest in my life, my thoughts, and my experiences. I couldn't help but feel a spark of curiosity and intrigue. In a time when human connection felt scarce and the world felt tumultuous, his consistent presence and attention provided a semblance of stability and comfort. Despite my initial reservations, the allure of someone showing seemingly genuine interest and understanding in such a trying period became difficult to resist. Maybe I *had* been wrong to brush him off. Maybe

I was shallow in judging him on his social media posts. I craved connection, and he seemed to offer it, even if it was within the confines of the digital landscape. As we continued to engage in conversation, we shared stories, laughter, and a sense of camaraderie that provided solace in those uncertain times. The virtual platform became our meeting ground, a space where we could bridge the physical distance and find solace in each other's presence, albeit through screens and messages.

As spring unfolded, so did a series of dates that ultimately led nowhere. I confided in him about my frustrations and letdowns. His counsel and a listening ear were comforting. After all, navigating the dating scene in New York City felt impossible. *I am losing so much time. I just want to meet someone normal! Are there any men left that know what they want? Fuck boi—Fuck boi—ugh what is the point. I give up.* As we fast-forwarded to the summer of 2020, a new chapter unfolded in our connection.The digital boundaries barriers seemed to melt away, and there we were, back in the familiar territory of the gym, but now training side by side. Before, our interactions had been fleeting, restricted to brief exchanges during class transitions or at gym events. But now, things felt different. I'd often catch sight of him coming in after his night shift, just as I was deep into my early morning regimen. There was this palpable sense of curiosity between us, as if our past virtual exchanges had kindled the spark for a deeper bond. While we were familiar faces from the gym, we had rarely ventured past casual greetings. He initially seemed shy and a bit tentative around me, but as our conversations grew, his guard began to lower. It wasn't the number of questions that made our talks memorable; it was his genuine interest in truly hearing my stories. He listened with intent, absorbing the depth and details of my experiences, gaining insights into the person I was beyond the edited glimpses on social media. Those gym interactions, which started almost as a continuation of our online rapport, went on to deepen our connection, exemplifying the beauty and strength of genuine, unfiltered communication. As our connection grew within the gym setting, there were other men I would engage in friendly conversations with. It was during these interactions that he would occasionally make side comments, jokingly referring to them as my "fans." At first, I found his remarks silly, not thinking much of them. I didn't perceive myself as someone who had "fans" in any conventional sense. *Is he trying to be funny? Also who says that? Weirdo.* In retrospect, I recognize a subtle red flag within those seemingly harmless comments. The mention of having "fans" hinted at possessiveness or jealousy lurking beneath the surface. While it may have initially come across as light-hearted "funny" banter, the comment held a deeper subtext that shouldn't have been overlooked. It revealed a certain level of possessiveness, suggesting a need to assert control or stake a claim over my interactions with others. Although I didn't grasp the significance of this observation at the time, it did serve as an early warning sign—a glimpse into the dynamics of our budding relationship. While engaging in our workouts together, I couldn't help but notice his persistent stares directed at me. It made me feel increasingly uneasy, prompting me to gently confront him about it. In response, he adamantly denied any such behavior, dismissing my concerns as mere imagination. *I see you, I feel you. I see you.* That is, until I presented him with a workout video of myself, where he was inadvertently captured in the background, his mouth covered by a towel, fixated on me. To my dismay, this pattern repeated in several other videos as well. He laughed it off, attempting to downplay the significance of his actions. However, the situation took an odd turn when he unexpectedly revealed that he was attracted to my scent. *My scent? Who says that?* Taken aback by his candid admission, I struggled to comprehend his explanation as he rationalized his behavior by citing pheromones and our "primal nature". This served as another red flag that I missed. The consistent presence of these red flags underscores potential boundary issues and a lack of respect for personal space. His persistent staring, coupled with his inappropriate explanation regarding attraction to my scent, should have raised concerns about objectification and objectifying language, suggesting problematic attitudes towards women.

These red flags, if realized, should not have been ignored or dismissed, as they provided foreshadowing into the dynamics of interrelations moving forward. *Mom always said that how you start is how you finish.* Despite my inner hesitations, I made a conscious choice to suppress my own feelings and dismiss the red flags that were waving before me. In an attempt to preserve the connection we *might* have had, I pushed aside my doubts and chose to prioritize the *idea* of a deeper bond over my own well-being. It was a decision rooted in the desire for connection and the fear of losing what I thought I might have found. *What a story. We met at the gym we both were members of for years. We were looking for love and it was right there under our nose the entire time. I think he is choosing me. The perfect story.* We began partnering up for workouts, and over time, we developed what I believed to be a deeper connection.

Love Bombs

Love bombing is a manipulative tactic used in psychological and emotional abuse, where a person will shower their target with excessive flattery, praise, and attention in an effort to manipulate them into a relationship. This tactic can take on many different forms depending on the individual, but it often involves intense compliments, gifts, and promises of a perfect future together. The ultimate goal of love bombing is to gain control over the target and keep them emotionally dependent on the abuser. This behavior is often an attempt to quickly overwhelm and win over the target, preventing them from fully getting to know the person or situation.

Initially, I didn't sense a strong connection or compatibility with him during our initial interactions outside of the gym. As we sat across from each other, I found myself grappling with feelings of boredom and a lack of shared interests. Our interactions felt disjointed, much like a car laboriously trying to find its gear- a tangible disconnect, a challenge in discovering common threads. His online persona sharply contrasted with the man I encountered in person. On social media, he exuded a crass and provocative bravado. Yet face-to-face, he often leaned into a self-deprecating demeanor. This glaring inconsistency puzzled me, prompting introspective queries about his true nature. I found myself wrestling with the question of which persona was genuine, and whether layers of his character remained concealed from view. *You know those uncomfortable jokes—kid-like humor? Just not my style—not intelligently funny—to me. Yet, he's telling me that I have no sense of humor. His jokes strike me as those of a simpleton. My grandmother always used that word. Maybe there is something more? Maybe he is hiding his pain through his humor? I think he is hurting inside. That makes me sad, here I am judging. Stuff it down.* His status as a father violated my personal dating rules. *I love kids. Ideally, my dream is to build a family with my partner. Where we experience all the "firsts" together. We figure it all out together.* Despite the nagging reservations in the back of my mind, I found myself willing to give it another try. Perhaps it was the looming shadow of isolation brought on by the pandemic, tugging at my heartstrings. With a shrug and a 'why not?' attitude, I found myself agreeing to a second date—a surprisingly bold move, considering it was a trip to the vineyards upstate. *I like boldness. He has guts. I like that.* The thought of spending hours with him, the possibility of awkward silences or a lack of chemistry, weighed heavily on my mind. Yet, yearning for a fresh experience and a dash of optimism, I took the leap. To my surprise, the day unfurled beautifully with our conversation gliding seamlessly. He seemed transformed, a stark departure from the image I had conjured based on our earlier interactions. As I look back, the beginning of the love bombing phase is evident. During this period, he skillfully employed tactics to seize my attention and win my heart. Those lingering looks, promises intricately woven with my own dreams and aspirations, seemed tailor-made to make me fall head over heels. I was swept into a whirlwind, feeling as though our dreams had miraculously converged, kindling a spark of hope and exhilaration. *Building a family. Having a country home upstate. Yes, weekends in the country!* At first glance, it felt charming, but an intangible unease lurked beneath. *Pause. Something's not right. Listen closely. Something is off.* My instincts blared alarm bells, nudging me to tread lightly, yet I found myself puzzled, unable to pinpoint the root of my apprehension. Rather than honoring these gut feelings, I rationalized them as mere jitters, remaining hopeful about the potential bond forming between us. But in doing so, I overlooked a vital red flag—the fourth one: my own intuitive sense. I was sidelining the most essential warning system I had: **my inner voice**. My intuition was guiding me, but I was too enthralled by the allure of what *could be* to listen. *This might be my time. I have been waiting so long to enjoy life with my person. This is it! I am being chosen.* I pushed my inner voice to the background, feeling pressured to find logical reasons for pulling away. In retrospect, I understand these gestures were deliberate efforts to forge an emotional bond and sway my feelings. This initial phase of love bombing was merely the beginning, laying the groundwork for a convoluted and stormy relationship that awaited. As our relationship developed, the amount of time he spent at my apartment began to increase. At first, his consistent company was a welcome change: shared meals, late-night conversations, and the warmth of companionship. But as days melted into weeks, I sensed the imbalance. Every healthy relationship requires space for both individuals to breathe and maintain their independence. His pattern of only leaving for work, due to his night shifts, and returning to my place each morning became a constant. Curious about this, I broached the subject of his living conditions. He revealed he had left his previous apartment to be with his father, providing support during the pandemic due to severe health concerns. This disclosure painted him in a noble light, portraying him as self-sacrificing and dutiful. Giving him the benefit of the doubt, I decided not to challenge our living arrangement. *Think and speak positively. Don't bring negative vibes!* After all, the idea of cohabiting, building a shared life, and having someone ever-present had its appeal. It resonated with my yearning for a committed partner, someone who would always be by my side. In hindsight, another significant red flag emerged, marking the fifth one I had missed. With the pandemic's shadow looming large, a pertinent question slipped my mind: If he had moved in with his father to care for him, who was looking after his father now? His claim of residing with me for his father's sake didn't align with reality. This oversight further underscores the reality of how emotions and our yearning for connection can sometimes blind us to glaring inconsistencies. As the weeks turned into months, his sense of entitlement over my personal space became increasingly evident. While my home has always been a familial gathering spot, he began to demonstrate discomfort with their presence. Initially, he was warm and welcoming, but around the fourth month, his demeanor shifted. His comments about needing sleep or his apparent annoyance during their visits became hard to ignore. The subtleties of his behavior deepened my unease: the incremental volume increase on the TV when they were around seemed a deliberate attempt to distance himself. But what truly caught me off-guard was his decision to discuss his ex's mother with mine. His recount of the former's frequent phone calls to her daughter not only felt out of place but also carried a hint of disdain. Such behavior began to challenge the boundaries of what was appropriate and respectful in our shared space. *Did I just hear what I think I heard? What is he doing? Does he think he is being subtle?* At the time, I was perplexed as to why he chose to divulge details about his ex's familial dynamics to my mother. In hindsight, such behaviors starkly underscore his possessiveness, his craving for control, and his brazen disregard for personal boundaries. When he aired his grievances about needing sleep or appeared visibly irritated by my family's presence, he was not merely expressing discontent. He was staking a claim, asserting dominance over a space that wasn't inherently his. Furthermore, discussing his ex's mother's habits with my own seemed less like casual conversation and more a veiled critique, potentially aiming to destabilize my bond with my family. Rather than confronting these red flags head-on, I found myself navigating around them, adjusting my family visits to accommodate his preferences. *Slight adjustments to keep everyone happy. Easy.* Blinded by my intrinsic desire to maintain harmony, I failed to recognize the shifting dynamics unfolding right before my eyes. My default mode has always been to adjust, to smooth out edges, to make everyone comfortable and content. Yet, while I was busy placating, my family saw through the facade. Recognizing the signs of his overbearing behavior, my mother and sisters silently rallied together. They resolved to monitor the situation closely, acutely aware of the looming shadow of his possessiveness. Their unwavering support and keen vigilance would soon become my lifeline as the narrative further unraveled.

Welcoming his daughters into my home for dinners and cocktail nights became a cherished tradition that we all looked forward to. Together, we would gather in the kitchen, preparing mouthwatering meals such as perfectly cooked steaks and delectable crab legs, infused with love and shared culinary expertise. The air was filled with the aroma of spices, the sound of laughter, and the clinking of glasses as we indulged in delightful cocktails, each sip a toast to the joy of being together. These moments were a tapestry of warmth, connection, and shared experiences that brought us closer as a family. Getting to know his daughters was a privilege. They were remarkable young women, each with their own unique personalities and aspirations. It was a pleasure witnessing the genuine bond they shared with their father and the unconditional love they reciprocated. As we sat around the dinner table, engaged in lively conversations, and exchanged stories, I witnessed the joy and pride that radiated from him. He transformed into a devoted and loving father, cherishing these precious moments with his daughters. These gatherings revealed a side of him that touched my heart and deepened my admiration for him as a parent. The interactions with his daughters allowed me to glimpse into a future filled with the possibility of a blended family. Their presence in our lives added richness and depth to our connection, solidifying the importance of family bonds and the potential for a shared journey ahead. I envisioned a future where we would continue to create memories, overcome challenges together, and nurture a loving and supportive environment for both his daughters and our growing connection. These moments fostered hope and ignited a sense of anticipation for the future, as we embarked on a path of building a life rooted in love, understanding, and the promise of a strong and interconnected family unit. We wanted to create meaningful experiences as a blended family, and one such adventure was taking one of his daughters to the gun range. It was a significant step in fostering a sense of unity and camaraderie. As we entered the gun range, we emphasized the importance of safety, responsible gun handling, and respect for firearms. Guiding his daughter through the experience, we provided her with valuable lessons, instilling a sense of confidence and empowerment. This shared activity not only deepened our bond but also allowed us to create lasting memories as a blended family, solidifying our commitment to supporting each other's growth and well-being.

Road trips to the Hudson Valley outlets became treasured getaways for us. These journeys offered more than retail therapy; they were a chance to marvel at scenic vistas, unearth hidden treasures, and celebrate our finds together. As we navigated the outlets, the joy of discovery and the satisfaction of a good deal intertwined, injecting spontaneity into our bond. Dining, especially our steakhouse expeditions, was another shared passion. Each meal was an adventure for our palates, with exquisite cuts of meat, delectable sides, and fine wines taking center stage. Amidst this culinary backdrop, our conversations flourished, punctuated by shared laughter and deeper connections. Every meal was an opportunity to weave lasting memories. Our bond was forged through more than just shopping and dining. Through our drives, shared meals, and thrilling activities, we didn't just find enjoyment in the surface-level experiences. They served as building blocks for our relationship, shaping the narrative of our connection. These moments of togetherness and shared adventure allowed us to discover the joy and adventure in each other's company, fostering a deeper understanding of what it meant to build a life together. They became symbols of our willingness to explore new territories, embrace spontaneity, and create lasting memories as we journeyed toward a future filled with love, understanding, and the promise of a strong and interconnected family unit.

The relationship I had with my godchildren held immense significance in my life, and my partner recognized and respected the value I placed on these connections. One day, he surprised me with a thoughtful suggestion: to take my pregnant friend and her son on a trip to the orchards upstate. It was a day filled with joy, laughter, and exploration as we ventured through corn mazes and enjoyed the beautiful surroundings. He took on the role of pushing the carriage and showering attention on the little one, showcasing his genuine care and affection. This experience brought me immense happiness, and the fact that it was his idea made it even more special.

During this period, I found myself navigating the delicate balance of dividing my time between the people I loved and exploring the depths of my new relationship. It was a time of discovery and growth, as I sought to nurture connections with my loved ones while also fostering the connection I had with him. The ability to share such meaningful experiences with both my godchildren and my partner created a sense of harmony and integration in my life. As I ventured through the corn maze with the little one and witnessed the genuine care he showed, I couldn't help but feel a sense of warmth and gratitude. This day served as a reminder of the beauty that can unfold when the different aspects of our lives intersect, when the people we love come together, and when we are able to create lasting memories as a united front. Balancing time and energy between various relationships can be a delicate dance, but moments like these allowed me to see the potential for a harmonious blend, where the love and care I had for each person could coexist and thrive. It was through experiences like these that I learned the importance of nurturing not only my romantic relationship but also the connections I cherished with my friends, family, and godchildren. The idyllic moments we shared during the trip to the orchards soon gave way to the emergence of subtle tensions within our relationship. *As I reflect upon those moments, it becomes painfully clear that I was the only one truly invested in the connections I thought we were forging. What I believed to be genuine shared experiences and a growing bond turned out to be nothing more than an elaborate deception. It was a masterful con, carefully crafted to manipulate my emotions and create the illusion of a deep connection. Oh, how I wish I had known the truth back then. This realization hits me with a wave of mixed emotions—disappointment, anger, and a profound sense of betrayal. I was unknowingly caught in a web of deceit, as the venom of the lies slowly began to paralyze me.* Roughly a month after our memorable day out, his discontent became apparent regarding the time I allocated to my other commitments and activities. He would occasionally drop comments about the infrequency of our evenings spent together, highlighting the need to treasure and reserve that time solely for us. Yet, given his night shifts, the reality was that by nine in the evening, I'd be on my own. These remarks sparked an inner conflict in me, pulling me in different directions. I deeply craved quality time with him. Past relationships had left me familiar with the pangs of insufficient attention and time, and I naturally longed for the closeness that comes from meaningful shared moments. There was something deeply reassuring about having someone who not just desired, but indeed expected such togetherness. The allure of a partner who not only valued our relationship but also actively carved out time for us was undeniable. Yet, I was steadfast in my belief in retaining independence and honoring the ties I'd formed with friends, family, and my personal interests. I'd seen firsthand how some become ensnared by romance, letting it eclipse all else, making their entire existence pivot around their significant other. I was resolute in not treading that path. My goal was a harmonious equilibrium: deepening my bond with him without sidelining the other passions and relationships that enriched my life. This juxtaposition of desires presented a nuanced inner conflict. While his attention was tantalizing, I was also drawn to retaining my autonomy and the diverse elements that completed my life's tapestry. It was a continuous, intricate ballet of fostering our bond while cherishing my unique identity.As tension mounted, I wrestled with notions of compromise, boundaries, and the essence of a healthy relationship. *Was it fair for him to demand so much of my time and focus? How could I reconcile my needs and desires with the expectations he set? After all, shouldn't a partner encourage the pursuits and commitments that bring joy?* Confronted with these questions, I delved deep into introspection, pondering my core values and aspirations in a relationship. Amidst the ensuing inner tumult, I discerned the pivotal role of transparent communication and mutual understanding in navigating such challenges. Armed with this insight, I seized a tranquil moment during dinner to broach a heartfelt discussion about the importance of individual space and nurturing connections outside our partnership. Unbeknownst to me, our conversation would swerve into unforeseen territory. As I began articulating my feelings and reservations, I perceived a change in his disposition—a palpable resistance, a noticeable retreat. It felt as though an insurmountable barrier had suddenly sprung up between us, stifling the potential for genuine understanding. Alarmingly, my words seemed to evaporate before reaching him, disappearing into an abyss of seeming apathy. To my dismay, instead of fostering a constructive exchange, he retaliated with heightened defensiveness and aggression, enveloping us in a thick air of tension and discomfort. *What's happening here? Whoa, whoa, whoa. We need to slow down.* My attempt to communicate my concerns was met with a defensive reaction, as if my words were being interpreted as an attack on his character. When I addressed his energy and tone, expressing my discomfort, he swiftly dismissed my feelings and labeled them as unreasonable and ridiculous. He accused me of manipulating the situation, insinuating that I was attempting to silence his thoughts and dismiss his perspective. His response left me bewildered and disheartened. I had entered the conversation with sincere intentions of fostering understanding and seeking common ground. My hope was to engage in an open and honest dialogue that would lead us toward a resolution benefiting both of us. Instead, I encountered resistance, a lack of empathy, and an unwillingness to acknowledge or validate my perspective. This encounter further deepened my confusion and left me questioning everything. *I may be many things, but manipulative? Certainly not. If anything I am too fair and too passive. Where is he going here? I have never seen this side of him. What is going on? Compromise looks and feels like me yielding to his demands.* That evening's conversation did not lead to the understanding I'd hoped for. Instead of a productive discussion, I was met with alarming reactions. My concerns were not met with acknowledgement but with threats of unwelcome changes if I didn't yield to his demands. The sudden introduction of threats deeply disturbed me, making it challenging to voice my feelings. Retrospectively, I see that these threats introduced a manipulative and coercive power dynamic, making me feel cornered and uncertain. The once fluid communication and mutual understanding had now been supplanted by an expectation of my unchallenged compliance. The initial intent of addressing differences and seeking a middle ground was overshadowed by the extinguishing of my voice and needs. The underlying message was clear: my concerns were secondary to his demands. This shift left me profoundly disturbed. *A healthy relationship should be built on a foundation of trust, respect, and open communication. It should provide a space where both partners feel heard, valued, and able to express themselves without fear of reprisal or manipulation. Stuff it down. He has inner work to do, maybe he is willing. Maybe this is a test for us? He is hurting remember. Stuff it down.* The sudden introduction of threats eroded our foundation of trust and respect, vital pillars of a meaningful relationship. Instead of cultivating an environment of mutual understanding, it birthed a climate of fear, dominance, and emotional coercion. Such threats have no rightful place in a nurturing relationship; they corrode the very essence of trust and safety that partners should share. They obstruct genuine connection and relationship growth. This experience underscored for me the significance of upholding my boundaries and self-worth. Nobody should be pressured to compromise their core values or mental well-being due to threats or manipulative tactics. Looking back, I am filled with a mix of sadness and shame as I admit that, during that particular period, I had an alarmingly low sense of self-worth. *You are not loveable. You are not enough. You are not worthy. They will never choose you. Stuff it down.* I became ensnared in a vicious cycle of tolerating and accepting unacceptable behavior, passively allowing the erosion of my self-worth. Unbeknownst to me, my own vulnerabilities and blind spots made me an easy target. During this period, I found myself navigating a delicate balance between honoring my personal desires and what he believed was best for our relationship. *Don't speak, listen. Maybe he has a point? Stuff it down.* It was a time of introspection and self-reflection as I worked tirelessly to find harmony between my individual needs and the collective needs of our relationship. As time passed, I became increasingly aware of the mounting red flags in our relationship. *It's important to emphasize that the abuse did not occur all at once or consistently. It was a gradual and calculated process. There were moments of genuine happiness and bliss, followed by sudden shifts and moments of turmoil. It was a pattern that seemed almost magical, where forgiveness and forgetfulness would temporarily overshadow the pain and confusion, only for the cycle to repeat itself. Throughout this cycle, I was unaware of the true intentions behind these actions, unable to fully grasp the manipulation and control at play. It was a deceptive dance that kept me in a constant state of uncertainty and prevented me from seeing the reality of the situation. I take responsibility for my role in enabling and tolerating behavior that I initially attributed to immaturity or past trauma. I recognize that my willingness to give the benefit of the doubt and make excuses for the other person's actions allowed the abuse to persist. However, it is crucial to draw a clear line between accepting accountability for my own choices and actions, and absolving myself of responsibility for the deliberate abuse inflicted upon me. I refuse to internalize blame for the intentional harm that was inflicted upon me by another individual. Abuse is a conscious choice made by the abuser, driven by their own distorted beliefs and unhealthy patterns. I will not shoulder the burden of his actions, but instead focus on my own healing, growth, and empowerment. Back to the narrative.* One evident manifestation of his controlling behavior was his reaction to my indoor bike riding. Despite my dedication to this exercise for over a year, he suddenly began expressing extreme disapproval. While I admit there were times when I might've ridden excessively, it perplexed me why this personal routine, especially during the constraints of the pandemic, so deeply bothered him. His desire for control didn't stop there. If I mentioned being preoccupied with work during remote sessions, he'd react with offense. It felt as if any instance when I wasn't immediately available to him was taken as a slight. These behaviors lit up the warning signs in my mind. Each instance served as a stark reminder that something wasn't right. Yet, as aware as I was of these red flags, reconciling my feelings with his unpredictable behavior felt like trying to solve a jigsaw puzzle with mismatched pieces. Despite clear warning signs, his problematic behaviors were often interspersed among our relationship's typical moments. Their sporadic nature allowed me moments of respite, leading me to downplay their seriousness or dismiss them. This dynamic perpetuated a cycle that kept me anchored in the relationship. Internally, I wrestled between recognizing these red flags and my attempts to rationalize them. Part of me yearned for explanations that fit the idealized relationship image I held, while another part instinctively felt that something was amiss. This discord made it difficult to fully confront the concerning dynamics. Eventually, I came to recognize how I had been conditioned to tolerate behaviors detrimental to my well-being. *See, I told you it would serve me incredibly well. Stuff it down. Good girl.* As I reflect on these past experiences, the seemingly isolated incidents from back then come together, revealing a consistent pattern of control and manipulation. While I initially dismissed or downplayed events such as his reactions to my indoor bike riding and work commitments, their cumulative effect becomes undeniable when viewed in conjunction. The common denominator throughout these instances was his need for control, intolerance for anything outside his expectations, and a proclivity to assert dominance through threats and aggression. These once-perceived isolated red flags now shine a light on the deeper, troubling dynamics of our relationship.

Future Faking

Future faking is a deceptive tactic commonly seen in relationships, where one person leads the other to believe in a future together by making grand promises, plans, and commitments that they have no intention of fulfilling. It involves creating an illusion of a beautiful and secure future, often playing on the hopes and dreams of the other person. This behavior can give the impression of a deep emotional connection and commitment, but in reality, it is a form of manipulation to keep the other person emotionally invested and hooked. The person who engages in future faking may use words, gestures, or even make concrete plans for the future, but they consistently fail to follow through on their promises, leaving the other person feeling betrayed, confused, and emotionally invested in a fantasy that will never materialize.

Within our circle, our relationship was often seen as an atypical union, leading some to dub us "the odd couple." Many friends, and even some of his family members, expressed their bewilderment about our pairing. To them, our dynamic was puzzling; they couldn't reconcile how someone like me, often described as a beacon of light and joy, could find contentment with someone perceived as his polar opposite. While they saw him as somewhat shadowed, I attributed those darker aspects to the scars of his childhood trauma. On several occasions, in private conversations, individuals shared their belief that I would eventually outgrow him. Some even made jesting remarks at gatherings, insinuating that there was still time for me to walk away from the relationship. Initially, I brushed off such comments, deeming them inconsequential. But as time unfolded and our relationship deepened, the weight of those words began to take on a different meaning. I began to wonder if I had been somewhat naive, perhaps overlooking certain facets of our relationship. My perception was that everyone around us accepted him—and our relationship—largely due to their affection and regard for me. The age-old saying comes to mind: "If you're happy, we are happy." He once confided in my sister that he had been drawn to me for a while. He expressed to my mother his disbelief and joy in being with me. To others, he voiced his intentions of wanting to marry. As our bond deepened, our conversations naturally drifted toward our shared dreams and hopes. Among all our aspirations, one stood out prominently: the mutual longing to have children. This was a non-negotiable for me, and I was overjoyed when he not only concurred but exuded genuine passion about the idea of parenthood. He wasn't reserved about this dream, openly discussing it with my sisters, my best friend, and even his daughters. Demonstrating his commitment, he considered consulting a fertility doctor, underscoring his dedication to the idea of building a family with me. His proactive approach was deeply reassuring. It provided a solid affirmation of our shared path and strengthened my conviction in our blossoming relationship. Our mutual dreams of parenthood not only drew us closer but also gave me the confidence that we were laying the groundwork for a lasting relationship, with a focus on creating a warm, loving home for our future offspring. *Little did I know that we would revisit this topic in the future, and that our perceptions and plans would be challenged in unforeseen ways.*

As time progressed, I began to notice a gradual shift in his behavior. His requests for my time and attention began to amplify. Initially, I interpreted the increased affection and attention positively, believing it allowed me to connect with a deeper, more intimate side of him, a side not exposed to others. The thoughts resonated: '*You are loved. You are wanted. You are chosen.*' However, as his demands grew, the balance tilted. I felt increasingly overwhelmed, bordering on suffocated. The equilibrium between our identities and our collective one as a couple began to erode. Personal passions, hobbies, and friendships outside our partnership faded as his hunger for my undivided attention seemed never to be satisfied. I was caught in a tug-of-war—yearning to nourish our bond while also maintaining my independence. Expressing my need for personal space without risking the foundation of our relationship became a challenge. In hindsight, beneath the surface of what seemed like genuine affection was a growing possessiveness, a desire to control. What initially felt endearing soon took a toll, revealing demands neither sustainable nor healthy. A heavy burden pressed upon me. Each thought weighed down: '*This is too much. I can't bear it any longer. It's suffocating. What's happening?*' Confusion clouded my mind. I found myself continually placing his needs above mine, sidelining my desires and dreams. To sidestep confrontations, I started curbing my authentic self, tailoring my words and actions to fit his mold. Our bond revolved around his dictates, from mundane car rides to significant future plans. My aspirations took a backseat, continually adjusted to cater to his preferences. This cycle of stifling my voice to maintain peace left me grappling with an unsettling imbalance and growing discontent. I increasingly felt that my identity was being diminished, my authentic self becoming a mere shadow. True relationships thrive on a delicate balance of individuality and collective experiences, where both partners voice their desires openly. Yet, our connection was morphing into a suffocating realm. I felt ensnared in a cage of his design, my aspirations and needs belittled. Any attempt to express my needs was met with resistance, further obscuring my sense of self. As I consistently catered to his desires, my dreams took a back seat. Personal passions, friendships, and my growth were neglected, and sacrificed to preserve our bond. It dawned on me that our dynamic was becoming oppressively one-sided. The more I labored to match his standards, the lonelier I felt, cut off from the vibrant activities and connections that once invigorated me. My diverse world narrowed, centering only on his wishes, resulting in a growing detachment from my identity. '*I yearn for my freedom, the simplicity I once took for granted. Why does this feel so challenging? Perhaps I'm not giving enough? I miss myself.*' We regularly ventured on weekend drives, exploring the Hudson Valley region's splendors. These trips, an escape from the urban hustle, immersed us in nature. At first, I cherished these escapades; they added layers of adventure and togetherness to our relationship. I reveled in uncovering the gems of unknown terrains, taking joy in every exploration with him. Yet, as our escapades continued, a subtle transformation became evident in the dynamics of our weekend outings. What began as carefree adventures started hinting at a concealed intent. The underlying tone of these excursions started taking on an isolating quality, gradually exposing a grimmer reality. It wasn't just about embracing nature's magnificence anymore; the trips increasingly served to disconnect me from my regular activities, family, and friends, rendering me unexpectedly unavailable. Moreover, controlling tendencies seeped into our daily lives, steadily eroding my autonomy. A particular point of contention emerged around my phone use. Any engagement with it seemed to evoke his irritation, as though my entire focus should be reserved for him. To sidestep disputes, I began concealing my phone and curbing potential distractions. What's more, though he had a functional phone, he'd often insist on using mine for GPS during our trips. At first glance, it might seem like a mere convenience. However, in time, I discerned it had a dual objective: it not only limited my access for extended periods but also granted him an opportunity to oversee my messages and alerts, encroaching on my privacy. These controlling actions chipped away at my self-assurance and freedom. They ushered in an atmosphere of perpetual wariness, compelling me to constantly gauge and adjust my behavior to avert his displeasure. In hindsight, these tactics were deliberate, meant to manipulate and diminish my independence. The erosion of my sense of self was gradual but persistent, as my autonomy and choices were stealthily encroached upon. As the pattern became more pronounced, an uneasy feeling grew within me. Those once-idyllic settings and charming landscapes lost their allure, only acting as stark reminders of my increasing detachment from the outer world. With every trip, I felt an ever-deepening chasm growing between me and my loved ones. I missed my friends. I missed myself. Amid this orchestrated detachment, he'd often reiterate, 'We are all we need.' This refrain's true implications began to dawn on me. It wasn't just a sweet sentiment but a means to rationalize our growing seclusion, a way to dissuade me from reaching out to friends and family. He was conditioning me to believe that our bond was paramount, effectively placing him above all else. When I confided in him about missing my friends, his response was unsettling. He accused me of being a neglectful friend and questioned my commitment to my relationships. I was taken aback. Thoughts raced through my mind: '*Isn't he the one who's been criticizing me for even thinking about events that don't revolve around him or his wants? How is this my fault? I am not a bad friend. Right?*' His words were a deliberate ploy, and they wounded me deeply. In a bid to restore some semblance of normalcy and connection, I decided to organize a wine-tasting. I meticulously arranged for themed plates, napkins, and hand-picked wines. I was all set to extend invites to my girlfriends. Yet, when I shared my enthusiasm with him, his objection was immediate and curt: 'Not in our house.' He further expressed his perplexity over why I'd want to do something for 'so-called friends' who he believed had deserted me. His contradictory stance left me reeling. '*Had he not just implored me to make more of an effort? And now when I do, suddenly my friends aren't worth it?*' His reaction was a crushing blow, obliterating my hopes of rekindling connections and fostering joy. It was becoming painfully evident that he viewed my friendships as an adversary, seeing them as entities beyond his sphere of influence and control. His refusal to permit the wine-tasting event at our home wasn't just about that particular occasion; it was a deliberate attempt to erode my relationships and enhance my reliance on him. Deep down, I was certain of one thing: my friends had always stood by me and would continue to do so, even if they couldn't fathom the intricacies of my relationship. Their unwavering support was something I valued deeply, and I wasn't going to let his words taint those bonds. Yet, at that moment, I was caught between my desire for social connection and his disparaging comments about my friends. I was engulfed in inner turmoil, battling between the fear of losing his approval and the yearning to rekindle ties with those who had been pivotal in my life. The wine tasting idea? I set it aside. Was he perhaps right? No, my friends cared about me. And I cherished them. Despite my genuine efforts to value time with my friends and family, he persistently set up barriers preventing me from enjoying those moments. In what seemed like clockwork, he'd disrupt these events with ceaseless phone calls, pestering me with inconsequential questions, and pressuring me to return home posthaste. If we had just parted, within what felt like mere minutes, my phone would buzz, signaling his impatience. I remember thinking, '*Where am I? I just left 30 minutes ago, I am where I was going. What is this?*' It was too much. The intensity was overwhelming, bordering on stifling. I always strived to be fully present when with loved ones, often immersing myself in activities that fostered joy and tranquility. To achieve this, I'd sometimes keep my phone out of sight, choosing to disconnect digitally and be entirely in the present. Yet, this very act, borne out of a desire for genuine connection, became a cause for his outbursts. Be it during a yoga session or a massage, where answering calls is naturally infeasible, he'd respond not with empathy but with ire. His incessant need for constant access, regardless of my situation, was taxing. Even slight deviations from his unrealistic expectations of immediate attention seemed to trigger a barrage of harsh words. The realization that I couldn't even prioritize my well-being without invoking his anger was disheartening. It was a clear testament to the control he sought over every facet of my existence, making me feel cornered and stifling my ability to establish meaningful boundaries. Missing his calls became a harrowing source of anxiety for me, dreading the inevitable fallout. His demands for instantaneous responses and meticulous explanations bred an atmosphere rife with scrutiny and tension. An unanswered call or an "unsatisfactory" reply would unleash a torrent of verbal abuse, often out of proportion to the actual circumstance. Anticipating his anger and processing its emotional aftermath made me obsessively monitor my phone, nervously watching for missed notifications. I felt imprisoned, constantly on high alert, tiptoeing around his volatile temper. It felt like perpetual surveillance, with zero tolerance for even the slightest oversight. This ceaseless demand for prompt accessibility, paired with my growing dread of his outbursts, distanced me further from the outside world. I was swallowed by the need to predict and meet his whims, neglecting my mental well-being and inner peace along the way. By wielding fear as his weapon, he anchored himself in a dominant position, coercing me into subservience. I deeply longed for the freedom to immerse myself in cherished moments, free from his omnipresent demands. Yet, his consistent intrusions left an indelible mark, casting a shadow over the joy and intimacy I sought. His tactics not only sapped the pleasure from these experiences but also sabotaged my ability to strengthen ties with friends and family. I found myself ensnared in an endless loop of tension and fear. The frequent disturbances and volatile reactions not only strained my relationships but robbed me of the genuine happiness inherent to those shared moments. As our car journeys progressed, he began openly expressing his disdain for my family and friends. Every caustic remark felt like a dagger, attacking the essence of those who had stood by me for years. *Where is this coming from? How do you go from liking everyone to now having a grievance with each of them?* I sought to address my concerns, fervently hoping for a constructive dialogue or some semblance of understanding. And yet, deep down, I knew it might be a futile effort. Every attempt met evasion and deflection. When I tried to genuinely share my feelings, he would either divert the conversation or trivialize my worries. This left me wondering if my emotions were too extreme or misplaced. His recurring dismissals made me feel invisible and undervalued. His frequent retort, "You always think you know better," seemed to assert that my feelings and apprehensions mattered little to him. Instead of fostering an open, understanding dialogue, he overpowered my sentiments, casting me into a whirlpool of uncertainty and self-questioning. His tactics blurred my grasp on reality. If only I had recognized the gaslighting then. By circumventing meaningful discussions, he stymied the possibility of any evolution or resolution between us. Rather than confronting the problems head-on, he deftly sidestepped responsibility, often turning the blame on me. This consistent evasion left me perpetually baffled and invalidated, doubting my perceptions and questioning my instincts. My mounting shame and embarrassment compounded the situation. The prospect of revealing the genuine nature of our relationship deterred me, as I feared others' judgments and potential misunderstandings. Expressing the nuanced reality felt daunting, especially knowing that the gravity of his actions and my endurance might be met with skepticism or disbelief. I felt isolated, bearing the emotional weight of the relationship in silence, grappling with an internal tumult of confusion. An unusual aspect of our relationship was his eerily empty phone, conspicuously lacking photographs, call logs, or messages. When I broached the topic, he rationalized it as a preference for minimalism—to minimize distractions and stay present. However, when I pressed further, sensing an incongruence, he grew defensive and short-tempered. Despite my internal alarms signaling that something was amiss, I chose to take his words at face value, suppressing my reservations. *Everyone has their quirks and peculiarities, including their approach to phone usage, and perhaps his choices simply differed from mine. Let it go . . .* As time unfolded, my discomfort deepened, transcending the puzzling void of his barren phone. It became a nexus of many unsettling behaviors and signs. I discerned patterns of control and manipulation that surpassed his overt possessiveness about my whereabouts. At the forefront was his relentless pursuit of power. His compulsion to dominate every facet of my life—my actions, beliefs, even my very feelings—became palpable. He consistently chipped away at my confidence, diminishing my accomplishments, and veiling insults as humor. These tactics steadily wore down my self-worth, seeding doubt about my value. His proclivity to override my boundaries and belittle my sentiments further exacerbated the strain. Whenever I voiced concerns or expressed needs, he either trivialized them, dismissed them as inconsequential, or cunningly deflected the focus back onto me, as if my feelings paled in significance to his whims and wishes. Another alarming tendency was his drive to alienate me from those I held dear. He cast aspersions on my friends, painting them as detrimental influences or insinuating they weren't truly invested in my well-being. His veiled warnings framed them as adversaries to our bond. Imperceptibly, I found myself retreating from those who had once been my pillars, severing ties that once offered solace and understanding. To compound matters, his emotional oscillations were erratic. There were moments when he exuded warmth and charm, lavishing praise and adoration. Yet, with jarring unpredictability, his demeanor would shift—morphing into fury or adopting an icy detachment. Navigating this tumultuous emotional terrain left me perpetually anxious, tiptoeing around him, fearful of what might unleash his next tempest. I yearned to reach out, to spill everything to my mother. Yet once the words are out, they can't be taken back. The thought of confiding in my sisters, and sharing with my friends, was both enticing and daunting. *No, not now. Maybe it's best to see how this situation unfolds.* I reminded myself that he's especially sensitive around the anniversary of his mother's passing. *Could this behavior be tied to that? Stuff it down.* The manipulation and control I endured brought with it a suffocating blanket of shame and embarrassment. This made it agonizingly challenging to unveil the stark reality of our relationship with anyone. In my confusion, I grappled with articulating the intricacies of what I was living through. Truth be told, I couldn't even discern the nature of my own experiences, much less convey them accurately to others. A lurking fear of judgment and misinterpretation held me back. *You are smart. Why are you enduring this?* The tug-of-war within me—between the need to share my experiences and the impulse to shield his reputation—erected barriers that prevented me from seeking the understanding and support I so desperately craved. The mysterious void in his phone stood as a stark reminder of the secrets and enigmas lurking within our relationship, adding layers of complexity to my quest for clarity.

Grooming

Grooming is a tactic where an abuser manipulates another to isolate them, making them dependent and vulnerable to exploitation. The manipulator may control various aspects of the victim's life, from their appearance to social interactions. In narcissistic grooming, the goal is to mold the victim's perception of the narcissist's identity and intentions. This strategy often precedes gaslighting and sets the stage for subsequent abusive behaviors. It begins by making the victim feel positive and secure before introducing more overt manipulation and control.

I find fulfillment in partnerships, cherishing the camaraderie and the chance to deeply understand my significant other. For me, relationships are a journey of mutual growth and support, with both partners aspiring to be their best selves. We don't depend on one another for joy but rather come together to revel in the happiness we each bring. The essence is to uplift each other, creating a nourishing bond where both individuals and the couple can flourish. However, as our bond deepened, his persistent negativity towards others became impossible to overlook. Time and again, he'd bring up the same old criticisms. No matter how often I told him I'd heard it before, he'd continue with his tales. I couldn't help but wonder, "What could he possibly say about me behind my back?" It was evident he held strong resentments towards nearly everyone, including close family and friends. In these situations, I often tried steering the conversation towards understanding, aiming to foster empathy. Yet, he remained fixated on his negative stances. What distressed me more was his readiness to divulge private and intimate details about his family and friend's lives. He seemed oblivious to the inherent trust and confidentiality of personal relationships. He appeared to relish these revelations, using them to dominate conversations and display superiority. Such breaches of trust, the sheer indifference to others' privacy, were profoundly disturbing. His behavior not only highlighted a lack of empathy but also hinted at his incapability of maintaining sincere relationships. The underpinning motive seemed to be a compulsion to wield power, utilizing personal secrets to belittle and control. This insight made me ponder the genuineness of our connection. If he could so effortlessly infringe on his family and friends' trust, where did our relationship stand? Such betrayals and boundary violations weighed heavily on my heart, propelling me closer to the stark reality of our situation. As time unfolded, the veneer he displayed to the world began to crack. Rather than the proclaimed jack of all trades, he seemed more a master of none, except maybe the intricate art of deception. His captivating tales and lofty promises, which I once took to heart, were unmasked as mere tall tales crafted to mislead and manipulate. His penchant for spinning these narratives aimed not to share truths but to mold perceptions and emotions for his benefit. These tales were strategically designed, not to reveal but to hide his true self. His capacity to make grand commitments was glaringly disproportionate to his ability to follow through. This imbalance sowed seeds of doubt regarding his reliability. I grappled with the reality of our bond, wondering if his assurances were nothing but hollow words devoid of true intent. As this realization took root, I couldn't ignore his persistent belittlement of others. What started as veiled comments gradually evolved into blatant expressions of contempt, especially towards those who ought to have been held in esteem. This growing disdain, combined with diminishing trust and frequent boundary breaches, enveloped our relationship in a palpable haze of toxicity. The more I saw, the more evident it became: our bond was anchored not in trust and respect but in deceit and inconsistency. *Does he even like me?* Each time I mustered the courage to confront his negative behavior, he adeptly deflected, placing the blame squarely on me. He seemed to possess an arsenal of manipulative tactics, each designed to shield him from accountability. My genuine concerns were brushed aside as overreactions or excessive sensitivity. Instead of engaging in genuine dialogue and seeking resolution, he opted to gaslight and invalidate my emotions. As the days turned to weeks and months, his aversion to responsibility became undeniable. Rather than own up to his actions, he projected his faults onto others, using their perceived flaws as a protective barrier. This consistent evasion of accountability deeply troubled me. Integrity and personal responsibility are cornerstones to becoming a wholesome and respectful individual. Observing his apathy towards these principles raised alarming red flags that went against my core values. Such glaring misalignments in principles aren't something I can easily ignore in any partnership. Typically, my instinct is to distance myself from those who shirk responsibility. Yet, I grappled with a gnawing cognitive dissonance. While one voice inside me sounded alarms about the relationship's erosion, another clung to the hope that I could guide him toward personal growth. I found myself torn between the stark reality of missing integrity and the hopeful aspiration for change, leaving me in a whirlwind of ambivalence and doubt. *You've invested so much time. You have invested so much of yourself. But maybe it is time to cut your losses now. Yes, cut my losses. Maybe? Stuff it down. He's been through a lot in his life. Let's give him some grace. Stuff it down.* Throughout our relationship, I noticed his frequent references to past relationships. He consistently cast his exes in a negative light, a focus that left me uneasy. I believe past relationships should be discussed with discretion and respect. However attempts to redirect these conversations were met with resistance. His persistence in speaking poorly of his exes, and the lack of self-reflection, left me wondering: would he speak of me in the same manner if our paths were to diverge? Curious to understand his perspective and foster communication,

I asked about lessons he'd learned from past relationships, hoping it might lead to mutual sharing and growth. His evasive response, though, deepened my concerns. It hinted at a reluctance to acknowledge past mistakes and grow from them, suggesting a pattern of deflecting blame and casting himself as the victim. This behavior, coupled with his portrayal of past relationships, started undermining the trust in our bond. I began to question if he had the tools and mindset to face conflicts healthily. Relationships inevitably face challenges, but the strength of a bond is tested by how these challenges are navigated. The accumulating doubts about his ability for open communication and mutual understanding chipped away at the foundation of trust and stability I value in a relationship. *The common denominator is you. Either you suck at picking partners or perhaps you are the horrible one. Don't judge. Don't judge. Stuff it down. Stuff it down.* I found myself actively observing and mentally cataloging his behavior, especially concerning his past relationships. I noted the actions or inactions of his exes and the consequences that ensued. Due to my innate self-awareness and attentiveness, I inadvertently internalized these observations, utilizing them as guides to circumvent similar issues in our relationship. I became adept at reading his body language, searching for subtle indicators of anger or distress. What I didn't realize then was that this might have been exactly what he had in mind. *One more story. Stuff it down. Take notes.* One particular story he shared remains vividly etched in my memory. He recounted a disturbing altercation with his youngest sister, during which tensions escalated to a point where she considered involving law enforcement. He admitted to contemplating physically assaulting her, only to be stopped by their mother. As he described the incident, his emotions were palpable, making it seem as though he was reliving the moment. I later realized he used this tale as a manipulative tool, casting himself as the victim and emphasizing his family's support for his side of the story. He aimed to assert dominance, control the narrative, and subtly deter me from ever thinking of seeking external help or involving authorities. In hindsight, this wasn't just storytelling—it was a strategic ploy. He presented himself as the wronged party while shifting the blame onto his sister. The very idea that he leaned towards physical aggression and justified it using family dynamics was deeply troubling. It revealed his willingness to manipulate, highlighting his disregard for the well-being of others. This was more than just a single story; it was a glaring indication of his pattern of behavior: manipulating narratives, controlling perceptions, and asserting dominance without concern for the repercussions on those around him. *Why is he telling me these things? Why is he always angry? I need to get out of here.* This tale should have served as a stark warning that I was entwined with someone driven by manipulation and self-interest. In retrospect, I lament the ignored red flags. Indeed, hindsight is a relentless teacher. Travel became another means of subtle control, underscoring the manipulative dynamics of our relationship. Before I began dating him, I loved the freedom of Airbnb stays, relishing the chance to enjoy local experiences. In May 2021, I enthusiastically booked a quaint log cabin and, as the date neared, we invited two other couples, dear friends of mine, to join the adventure. But, with only two weeks left to our getaway, his demeanor changed dramatically. Seemingly trivial issues escalated into full-blown arguments, and he suddenly voiced his desire to cancel the trip. Worse, he declared that he didn't wish to continue our relationship, dashing my enthusiasm and leaving me feeling deeply embarrassed. Overwhelmed, I confided in my friends, subsequently canceling our plans. They offered immense understanding and comfort, reminding me that such hurdles are a part of life. Yet, just as I was coming to terms with this change, he did an about-face, wanting to reconcile and revive our trip plans. His unpredictability left me stunned. *I had already informed everyone that the trip was off, and I canceled the reservation. He knows this.* The sudden twist was both bewildering and vexing. Yet, wanting to make the best of it, I liaised with the cabin's owner and managed a rebooking. My friends, ever supportive, were still keen on joining. Their steadfast understanding eased my sense of embarrassment, reinforcing the idea that life is unpredictable. They urged me to concentrate on the trip's potential joys rather than dwell on past misgivings. And so, with a mix of hope and trepidation, we embarked on our journey, which, against the odds, turned into a wonderful escapade filled with love and joy. Opting to set aside the recent unsettling events, I immersed myself in the cherished moments of our shared adventure. *Stuff it down. Let it go.* I was initially unaware that this would become a recurring tactic in our future trips. He repeatedly attempted to exert control in this manner. From Jamaica to Turks and Caicos, and the Finger Lakes, he tried to sow doubts and uncertainties, aiming to derail our plans. However, after the ordeal surrounding my birthday at the log cabin, I vowed not to let him manipulate my travel experiences. I firmly communicated that if he opted out, I'd still proceed with the trips I had carefully arranged and financed. His surprise was palpable, especially regarding the Jamaica trip which involved his extended family. Nonetheless, I stood my ground, reassuring him of my intent to enjoy the journey, with or without him. Turks and Caicos held personal significance for me, having visited it alone previously. It was, therefore, an apt destination for a solo sojourn, a chance to rekindle my bond with the island and myself. As for the Finger Lakes trip, designed to celebrate his birthday, I deferred to his choices, responding with, "As you wish." Despite the uncertainty he tried to weave into our plans, each journey materialized as intended. Over time, I believe he refrained from this tactic, recognizing my willingness to embrace solo adventures and my staunch independence. Moreover, since I managed both the logistics and finances of our trips, he lacked the means to obstruct them. I owe much of this agency to my career and financial autonomy, which allowed me to steer my course. Yet, it's crucial to acknowledge that while I discerned these manipulative travel tactics, I was less perceptive of them in other facets of our relationship. In hindsight, the games played around our trips were merely a segment of an extensive pattern of control and abuse that spanned our entire relationship.

Sexual Narcissism

Sexual narcissism refers to a self-centered and self-enhancing attitude towards sex and sexual relationships. It involves an excessive focus on one's sexual prowess, seeking validation and gratification while disregarding the needs and boundaries of partners. It may involve manipulative behaviors, objectification of partners, and a lack of empathy.

Our relationship began with what seemed like innocent displays of affection. However, it quickly morphed into an unsettling and coercive dynamic. His disregard for my boundaries was suffocating, irrespective of whether we were in a private or public setting. More troubling was his blatant disrespect for my comfort and consent. Forceful and unwarranted physical advances, treating me as an object devoid of autonomy, became commonplace. At first, I tried to rationalize his actions as mere clinginess or insecurity. But it wasn't long before I recognized a deeper, more concerning pattern. When I mustered the courage to articulate my discomfort, emphasizing that his forceful grabs, especially of my breasts and butt, felt violating and far from affectionate, he reacted with indifference. It seemed as though my feelings and experiences were inconsequential to him. To compound the issue, he often resorted to the silent treatment as a punitive measure. Instead of addressing concerns through transparent communication, he would emotionally withdraw, using silence as a manipulative tool. This tactic only amplified the isolation and distress I experienced in our relationship. *What am I doing wrong? I am not comfortable, I should be able to voice that. Am I wrong? Maybe I am not used to this type of affection. This doesn't feel like affection. His actions are very animalistic.* Despite my ongoing efforts to assert myself and set boundaries, he consistently disregarded my personal space. It felt as though my attempts to stand up for myself only spurred him to push boundaries further, undermining my feelings and autonomy. His behavior, already invasive, intensified over time, leading to escalating anxiety and distress for me. The incessant violations made me feel objectified and devalued, as though I were merely an object of his possession rather than a partner deserving of genuine affection and respect. *This seems wrong. Wrong on so many levels. I have never been with anyone who did not engage with me lovingly and mutually.* In addition to his invasive behavior, he used manipulation to distort my sense of reality. Despite our frequent intimate encounters, he would accuse me of constantly rejecting him if I ever declined or expressed discomfort. This strategy created a perplexing contradiction, making it challenging for me to assert my boundaries without guilt. He consistently shifted expectations and invalidated my feelings, which was emotionally exhausting. His manipulation extended to our intimate life. Instead of striving for a mutual connection, he prioritized his desires, neglecting the importance of mutual consent. He would belittle me with derogatory comments and comparisons to past relationships. These tactics were intended to erode my confidence, aiming to establish a power imbalance. This continuous gaslighting affected my mental well-being, leading me to question my feelings and diminish my self-worth. It became a relentless cycle of psychological abuse that ensnared me in a web of persistent self-doubt. Within this manipulative and coercive environment, I started questioning my capacity to articulate my feelings and, over time, began shouldering the blame for his actions. *What am I doing wrong? Maybe he is right? Do men need more sex than women, I don't think that is a fact. Maybe this is what he needs? How much more can I give?* When he threatened to withhold all physical intimacy, I found myself bending under the weight of his demands, apologizing, and unknowingly perpetuating a detrimental cycle. This deepened feelings of entrapment and coercion. Beyond our interactions, his obsessive need for control manifested glaringly in the realm of social media. It was obvious that he meticulously observed my online actions, scrutinizing each post and even challenging my virtual engagements with others. This insistent surveillance was more than unsettling—it was invasive, attempting to dictate not just my real life but also my digital identity. His actions stripped away my sense of autonomy and fostered an omnipresent feeling of being monitored. This wasn't merely about control within the boundaries of our relationship; it expanded into a pervasive digital surveillance that isolated me further. I began to feel the weight of his watchful eyes on every online interaction, leading to an internalized censoring of my posts out of fear of his reaction or criticism. Initially, I mistook this behavior as a misguided expression of concern, rooted in his self-professed traumas from childhood. However, with time, I recognized it for what it truly was—a tactic to restrain my freedom. This behavior is hard to comprehend. What's truly at the heart of the matter? We originally connected through social media, and I've remained consistent in who I am. Under the pretense of protecting his privacy, he curtailed my self-expression and interactions with others. He used this rationale to excuse his behaviors, notably his intentional omission of photos of us together on his social media accounts. It became evident that he was deliberately keeping our relationship out of the public eye, crafting an image as though he was single. Later, I'd come to understand that those continuously seeking new attention and validation often use this approach to obtain new supply. If sharing a simple exercise is revealing 'personal business', then the bar is set quite low. Contrary to his belief, most people aren't as engrossed in my posts. Yet, he framed my online activity as oversharing, enveloping me in a cloud of shame and guilt. I adjusted, hoping to mitigate his concerns: by posting less frequently and curating my content more carefully. I believed this might ease his anxieties and foster harmony. But his critiques remained, paradoxically claiming I sought validation despite my noticeable cutback. His remarks about my social media behavior were inconsistent. While I worked to address his concerns, he feigned obliviousness to my efforts. It is now clear that his underlying motive was control, aiming to pull me away from broader connections. His rebukes left my self-confidence shaken, causing me to second-guess my actions. In a move that seemed to be a bid for control, he even blocked me on social media. Ironically, this meant he couldn't monitor my posts. Tensions peaked when he vehemently opposed me sharing workout photos in sportswear, even though this had been my practice long before our relationship. *I don't have to explain myself to anyone. I am allowed to post whatever I want.* Posting those images was a celebration of my journey. His persistent attempts to alter my behavior weren't rooted in concern but were clear efforts to control my narrative. I took a stand, making it unequivocally clear that this was not a topic open for negotiation. Despite this, he escalated matters to the absurd, even threatening to destroy my sports bras. My stance remained unyielding: his threats wouldn't change my conviction. I saw past his manipulative ploys in the realm of social media, unwilling to let his intimidation shape my online interactions. However, I remained somewhat oblivious to the broader spectrum of control he exerted in our relationship. His excessive reactions to minor issues left me bewildered, prompting me to ponder why such inconsequential matters triggered such disproportionate outbursts. It's puzzling how an adult could exhibit behavior reminiscent of toddler tantrums. Just when I grappled with his demanding nature, he'd conveniently share stories from his traumatic childhood. Tales of how his father physically abused his mother and brought a tempest of drugs and anger upon the family. His vulnerability, paired with these heart-wrenching accounts, often made me sympathize with him. He would subtly leverage these stories, suggesting that his actions were consequences of his traumatic past, thereby shifting blame. This painted a picture where holding him accountable seemed unjust, given his past suffering. Such tactics, I've come to understand, are frequently employed by abusers to sidestep responsibility. Narcissists masterfully control through insidious manipulation, conditioning their victims into subservience. They craft an atmosphere where their mandates are unchallenged, and defiance appears insurmountable. I found myself relinquishing passions to evade his ire or the aftermath of not meeting his standards. Having never encountered abuse as an adult, I couldn't spot the red flags or discern the manipulative strategies at play. This blind spot rendered me susceptible. It's crucial to note, however, that the onus of abuse lies with the abuser. Victims cannot be faulted for not seeing signs immediately, especially when abuse often manifests in veiled, elusive ways. Looking back, a pang of regret and self-reproach hits me, realizing how long I stayed in that toxic relationship. There were moments, more than I'd like to admit, when I yearned to leave. But I was ensnared in the belief that I was alone in this and somehow deserved what I was enduring. With clarity now, I see how deeply the manipulation and gaslighting had affected me. I deeply wish I had sought help or confided in someone about the ordeal. But that's the nature of abuse—it often isolates and silences its victims, making them feel trapped and alone.

Gaslight

Gaslighting is a deeply harmful form of emotional abuse that aims to manipulate and control the victim by distorting their perception of reality. The term "gaslighting" originates from a play and subsequent film adaptation called "Gas Light," where a husband deliberately manipulates his wife into questioning her sanity. This psychological manipulation is designed to make the victim doubt their experiences, memories, and even their sanity, thereby granting the abusive partner even more power and control.

As the early evening moonlight bathed the living room, I cherished a quiet moment of solitude, engrossed in my phone—likely lost in Instagram's pull. He seemed at peace, sleeping in the bedroom, and I welcomed the calm before his upcoming night shift. Out of nowhere, he emerged, startling me so abruptly that I nearly lost grip on my phone. I couldn't have imagined that this fleeting moment would be twisted into the foundation for our first contrived argument. Almost immediately, he transformed, hurling accusations, insisting that my sudden alarm and phone use were clear indicators of infidelity. *Is this actually happening?* My mind was reeling from the sudden and baseless accusation. In an earnest attempt to ease his suspicions, I offered my phone as proof. But it was as if a switch had been flipped within him. He transformed, veering from tranquil to tempestuous in an instant. I was left grappling to make sense of the situation; I'd never encountered such a volatile outburst before, let alone been accused of infidelity—a concept utterly foreign to my nature. His tirade persisted, spilling into the night through endless calls and texts, only to cease abruptly at three in the morning. This distressing pattern would consistently manifest itself shortly before his night shifts. Each confrontation, while varying in specifics, had the central premise: he believed I took pleasure in his emotional turmoil. "You love seeing me like this," he'd spit out. These confrontations often climaxed in drawn-out late-night calls, his voice spewed with anger and blame. Any attempt to cut the conversation short would only amplify his rage, leading to more menacing threats. I found myself absorbing these outbursts in silent endurance, waiting for his rage to subside. And when he'd seemingly exhausted his anger, he'd disingenuously inquire, "Do you want to talk?" Aware that this was merely a bait to prolong the conflict, I consistently chose not to take the bait. This recurring pattern was not just about venting frustration—it was a calculated move to diminish my autonomy and solidify his dominance. *Stuff it all down. Just be silent. Stuff it down.* The repeated pattern of fabricated conflicts and emotional turmoil left me disoriented and hurt. I found myself incessantly trying to decipher the reasons for his volatile behavior. Could he be on unknown medication? Or perhaps grappling with an undisclosed mental condition? Ironically, despite his claims of hating to walk on eggshells during his childhood, I felt trapped doing just that—constantly wary of igniting another outburst. Throughout our relationship, he would deliberately provoke me, only to later refute any wrongdoing. He twisted events and denied words he clearly uttered, making me question my memory. Even more bewildering was his capacity to shift from agitator to caretaker in an instant. He would unsettle me, then play the comforting role, seemingly enjoying the act of "resolving" issues of his own making. His assurance that he was my sole protector and pillar of strength left me stunned and drained. *What a mindfuck. One exhausting mind fuck. I don't know how much more of this I can bear.* The alternating dynamics of causing distress and then offering comfort served his purpose of perpetuating a sense of chaos in our relationship. *Did I say what I thought I said or did I say what he said I said?* I became trapped in a web of confusion, questioning my sanity and constantly second-guessing the reality of every situation. *What is this? What am I doing wrong? I can't mention this to anyone. I will seem crazy for enduring this. Am I crazy for enduring this? I AM crazy for enduring this. This doesn't feel normal. Maybe I should call someone. No. How will you look? Maybe therapy? Is something wrong with me? Stuff it down. Yes, therapy. Stuff it down.* In addition to the emotional manipulation and control in our conversations, there were instances when he would weaponize car rides as a means to instill fear. These experiences were nothing short of terrifying, characterized by intense tension and unpredictable outbursts. During his eruptions, he would purposefully drive recklessly, engaging in dangerous behaviors such as speeding, swerving through traffic, and displaying aggressive physical actions like punching the steering wheel while screaming. Simultaneously, he would unleash a torrent of hurtful words, berating and belittling me. In those moments, it felt as though he was intentionally putting our lives at risk, using the car as a tool to intimidate me. The combination of his erratic driving and verbal abuse created an environment of extreme fear. *Just stare out the passenger window. It will be over soon. Don't move your head, don't say a word. Stuff it down. Stuff it down.* I would constantly brace myself for the next explosion, unsure of how far he would take it. The constant fear and uncertainty during these rides left me emotionally shaken and physically on edge. *Hide your shaking. It will only enrage him more. Take it. Stuff it down.* When I voiced my discomfort, he intensified the situation—raising his voice and driving even more recklessly. It seemed he relished my fear, using the car as a tool of intimidation. These rides mirrored the overarching power imbalance in our relationship, making me feel as trapped as I did during our phone calls. It was another strategy in his arsenal, aimed at ensuring my submission and compliance. By instilling a perpetual state of fear, he solidified his control over me. Reflecting on it now, I see the profound toll these abusive car rides took on my emotional and psychological well-being, deepening the scars and widening the chasm of trust.

Triangulation

The narcissist may use the presence or interest of a third party as a means to exert control, create insecurity, and manipulate their partner's emotions. By introducing the idea of a threesome, the narcissist aims to exploit their partner's fears, desires, and insecurities, pressuring them into participating in sexual acts that go against their boundaries or wishes. Triangulation in this context is a harmful and abusive behavior that disregards the autonomy and consent of the partner, focusing solely on the narcissist's gratification and control.

He had a knack for creating drama out of nowhere, and it was unpredictable. One incident that stands out occurred in Mystic, CT, during the holiday season. The town was teeming with people, and the crowds began to overwhelm me. Hoping to ease my discomfort, I suggested we choose a less busy spot to eat. But he resisted, insisting we check every restaurant on Main Street. All the while, he peppered in snide remarks, hinting that I believed I was above everyone else. *What?* His accusations surprised me. I never saw myself as superior to anyone; I just desired a quieter dining spot. I thought I was simply sharing my preference. However, rather than trying to understand or discuss it constructively, he chose to publicly berate me right on the street. *This is different. Usually, this is done in private. What is happening?* Frozen with embarrassment, I couldn't defend myself against his barrage of false accusations and belittlement. It was a humiliating ordeal. I had always believed in treating my partner with respect, never demeaning them, especially not publicly. Thankfully, our favorite restaurant had a table ready, providing a brief reprieve from the scene he had caused. We ate in silence. He didn't speak for the rest of the day until we crossed into Westchester County. *Keep staring out the passenger window. Don't move. Don't use your phone. Stay still and silent.* Suddenly, in a calm tone, he revealed something unexpected. He mentioned a woman from the gym who wanted to join us for dinner or drinks that evening. He said they'd been chatting during their workouts and described her as "super cool." *To clarify, he had frequently broached the idea of a threesome, often interjecting it during intimate moments as foreplay. While I hadn't given a definite answer, I mentioned that I might contemplate it under the right conditions. However, I never actively pursued this, as I inherently prefer monogamous relationships.* In that instant, all the pieces fell into place. It felt as though the floodgates had burst open. I recognized that the earlier altercation in Mystic was likely a tactic he used to create a plausible reason to "need space" upon our return. If he wanted to venture out alone, this would provide the perfect excuse for him to disappear. Furthermore, he seemed to be using triangulation to manipulate me into acquiescing to his desires. *I did not know that word at the time but the outcome is still the same.* The accusations, belittlement, and public humiliation were tactics he used to manipulate me, attempting to pressure me into agreeing to something outside of my comfort zone. My mind raced, feeling a palpable manipulation suffocating the atmosphere in the car. We drove in tense silence until he suddenly announced we'd pick her up en route. As she climbed in, I was immediately overcome with unease. He greeted her by mentioning her toe, referencing an accident at the gym where a woman had injured herself with a dumbbell. Both he and I had seen this incident. But it quickly became clear that this wasn't the same woman. Everything from her physical appearance to her hair was different. She seemed baffled, claiming no knowledge of any toe injury. Yet, he kept pressing her about it, becoming more frustrated with each of her confused denials. The scene unfolding before me only deepened my sense of unease and raised unsettling questions about the truth and intentions behind his words. *Is he really telling her that she was the woman who dropped a weight on her toe? I think she would know. This is insane. I am witnessing a literal definition of insanity right now.* This inconsistency was just one of many puzzling elements that failed to align and raised further suspicions. Once we got settled in, things seemed somewhat normal on the surface. I tried to engage in light conversation, attempting to create a comfortable atmosphere. However, there was still an underlying feeling of something being off, especially since I'd been told she wanted to spend time with both of us. Throughout dinner, her tension was palpable, and there was an undeniable unease in her eyes as we discussed life. *Something is very wrong here.* Her eyes seemed to bear a hidden burden. Sensing her unease, I suggested wrapping up the evening, offering her an easy exit. She quickly agreed. When her Uber arrived, he rushed to escort her, while she seemed eager to distance herself from him. The night ended, bringing relief that things hadn't escalated. Yet, the silent tension lingered, leaving me with an uneasy feeling and many unanswered questions. Much later, I uncovered the truth about the woman who was in the car. It turned out that she had been a survivor of domestic violence, and she had shared her experiences with him in great detail. The revelation shook me to the core and left me deeply disturbed. It became clear that he had deliberately concocted a false background story about her, possibly to manipulate me, incite jealousy, or instill a sense of competition. The extent of his deceit made me want to vomit. The fact that he would exploit someone's incredibly painful past for his gain revealed the depths of his callousness and complete absence of empathy. It was a betrayal not only to me but also to the woman who had trusted him with her story. It was a disturbing revelation that showcased his willingness to distort the truth and fabricate narratives to suit his agenda. As I reflected on this incident, it became clear that his manipulative behavior was not isolated but rather a consistent pattern that permeated all of his interactions. *I want out. Stuff it down. Stuff it down.*

Fade to Black

By April of 2021, our relationship had become an exhausting rollercoaster ride of unpredictable emotions. He had developed a troubling pattern of initiating frequent breakups whenever he didn't get his way. Initially, each threat to leave and move out would devastate me. However, as time went on, I grew numb to these manipulative tactics, knowing that he would inevitably reconcile by the next morning, pretending as though nothing had happened. This twisted routine left me feeling emotionally drained. What made it even more disorienting was how he would completely erase the memory of these painful episodes once he reconciled. It was as if he had selective amnesia, conveniently forgetting the turmoil he had caused. His blank stare and dismissive attitude, when I tried to address the issue, made me feel invisible and invalidated. I was left to grapple with the emotional fallout on my own, while he effortlessly moved on, unwilling to acknowledge the impact of his actions. It took me a while to realize that this cycle of breaking up and making up was a deliberate tactic to exert control and drain my energy. He thrived on the power dynamics created by these emotional rollercoasters. The emotional abuse I endured was intensified by his rapid and extreme shifts in his perception of me. One moment, he would idealize me, treating me as the perfect partner and showering me with affection and praise. But in the blink of an eye, he would suddenly demonize me, accusing me of imagined transgressions and projecting his insecurities onto me. This constant whiplash of his changing attitudes and behaviors left me in a constant state of anxiety. *I think I have had my fill. I think I deserve better. I deserve more. I deserve love and respect.*

Catch-22

Our relationship dramatically changed when he had a heart attack at the gym on April 28, 2021. By sheer coincidence, I was present and intervened, performing CPR until emergency services arrived, as no one else present was able to take proper action. *Ironically, he had broken up with me the evening before and was giving me the silent treatment that very morning.* Doctors later confirmed that without my actions, he would've either died or sustained severe brain damage. The magnitude of this event weighed on me, and I felt a profound sense of duty towards his well-being. Consequently, I transitioned into a caregiver role, dedicating endless hours to his recovery. I remained steadfast by his hospital bed, catering to his needs and providing emotional comfort. During this period, I observed a marked change in his behavior. He appeared genuinely appreciative of my efforts, treating me with what appeared to be authentic newfound kindness and affection. It gave me hope that perhaps this near-death experience had prompted him to reevaluate himself and make lasting positive changes. In an attempt to salvage some hope and understand his mindset, I confronted him about the significance of this second chance at life. I asked if he viewed it as an opportunity to approach his life differently, a chance to prioritize love, respect, and growth. The response I received was soul-crushing. He looked me dead in the eyes and bluntly said, "No." It was a moment of brutal honesty that shattered any illusions I had held onto. As we faced the aftermath of the heart attack, our relationship was filled with heightened tensions and silence. He consistently voiced a desire for space, leaving me to confront the lingering effects of the incident on my own. Flashbacks of that critical moment haunted me, bringing forth a rush of overwhelming emotions that I struggled to process. The dynamic between us shifted drastically. The once-present appreciation in the hospital seemed to fade into the background, replaced by a palpable distance. It felt as though an invisible barrier had formed between us, isolating our individual experiences. I yearned for open communication and mutual support during this trying time, hoping that we could come together to heal and find solace in each other's presence. However, his insistence on withdrawing and creating emotional distance left me grappling with feelings of confusion, loneliness, and a deep sense of isolation. *Who can I talk to that can understand? Why can't he be here for me?* During this vulnerable time, I chanced upon an unfamiliar name in a notification on his phone. *I think he mentioned her before, but I was sure it was mostly negative.* Compelled by a blend of suspicion and curiosity, I delved deeper. My heart sank as I unearthed messages revealing his engagements with *multiple* women, extending beyond mere friendship. *Explicit photos.* The proofs sprawled across texts, social media, and WhatsApp, causing my body to tremble uncontrollably. Summing up the courage, I contacted one of these women, who candidly divulged what she knew. This revelation struck me deeply, magnifying the sense of betrayal and annihilating the residual trust I had clung to. It was a painful confirmation that the person I had saved, the person I had dedicated myself to caring for, was engaging in deceitful behavior behind my back. The weight of this knowledge brought a surge of conflicting emotions—anger, hurt, and a profound sense of disillusionment. *Control your shaking. Don't scream. Don't cry. Stuff it down. Stuff it down. Put it together.* The day we returned from the hospital, he made it clear that he needed some time alone to fix the car's headlights. He specifically requested that I stay home, accusing me of suffocating him and treating him like a child. Although his words stung and left me feeling hurt and confused, I respected his request and tried to give him the space he seemed to desire. As I waited anxiously at home, my mind was plagued with doubts and questions. Something felt off, and

I couldn't shake the unease that settled within me. It was on this day, that she revealed that they had slept together, May 4th, 2021, "as they often did at her place". *Often. Often. Often. Often. Often is an adverb meaning frequently, many times. Often. Stuff it down.* The ground beneath me seemed to crumble as the weight of his betrayal crashed down upon me. The truth of his infidelity hit me with an intensity I had never experienced before. It was as if the walls of our relationship, already weakened by the abuse and manipulation, came barreling down, leaving me in a state of profound despair and disbelief. My world was engulfed in darkness. Waves of pain, anger, and sadness crashed over me, threatening to pull me under. I felt an overwhelming sense of powerlessness, everything I had believed in had been confirmed to be an illusion. *He accuses me of cheating because he has been cheating this entire fucking time. I am having PTSD from saving his life and he's fucking around texting exes and random women. He lives in my house. I pay for everything. Everything. This is insanity. Why would she lie? Why would she lie? Why would she lie? Stuff it down. Stuff it down. Stuff it down. She wouldn't lie, would she? Stuff it down. Stuff it down.* With sincere gratitude, I thanked the woman for her honesty and for revealing this painful truth. I understood internally that she wasn't at fault. He had deceived both of us: leading her to believe he was single and living with his father, while assuring me of our exclusive, committed relationship. *He even went so far in the beginning of his courtship to go out of his way to say that he ended it with everyone he was talking to as he did not want to risk losing me. I am a fool.* While we were on our way to his uncle's house for their Memorial Day BBQ upstate I decided to confront him about the other woman, and all the messages I read, seizing the opportunity while we were waiting in the car for his family to join us. I was calm and collected, as I mentioned her name, I watched his face go pale, a clear sign that he had been caught in his web of lies. Attempting to maintain his composure, he denied any wrongdoing and vehemently insisted that *she* was lying. Admitting to seeing her, he claimed that their interactions were innocent and that he had only dropped by to say hello since she lived near the autobody shop. However, the weight of his betrayal was palpable in the air. He was caught in his web of deceit, he was unable to explode in anger due to the imminent arrival of his family, nor could he flee from the situation. Disgust coursed through me as I listened to his feeble attempts to justify his actions and tear her down. The trust I had placed in him had been shattered beyond repair. I could no longer bring myself to believe his words or entertain the possibility of his innocence. The evidence and the depth of his deception were too overwhelming to ignore. My heart and mind were filled with a mixture of anger, disappointment, and a profound sense of disgust at the person he had revealed himself to be. I never looked at him the same way. From that moment forward, I could never look at him in the same way. While part of me tried to rationalize the situation, attributing it to the stress of his heart attack and questioning the credibility of the other woman's claims, I could never fully put back on the rose-colored glasses he had once convinced me to wear. *Why would she lie? Why would she lie? Why would she lie? Why would she lie? Why would she lie? You never died and came back to life, maybe he just had a moment? Why would she lie? Stuff it down.* I told my mother. *Finally, I told someone something.* Just a little piece but enough to feel a little free. She did not judge. She listened. She said to listen to my gut and to do what I needed to do. She emphasized that saving his life didn't obligate me to stay with him. *She is right. But for some reason, I can't seem to want to walk away, just yet. Am I addicted to this toxicity? Do I need more proof than the mountain standing in front of me? What is wrong with me? I would never entertain this. I would never tell a friend to entertain this. What is happening? What is wrong with me?* For a few months, or perhaps even several, he seemed to behave or, more accurately, became more skilled at concealing his behavior. I couldn't ignore the increasing amount of time he spent engrossed in his phone and social media. *Everything at the beginning of our relationship, especially his fixation on my phone and social media, was becoming more and more clear. I became a silent observer, witnessing it all unfold before my eyes.* Text messages to his exes, explicit photos, and call logs revealed a truth I couldn't deny. I took screenshots, capturing undeniable evidence of his deceit. *Whenever I needed to ground myself I would scroll through them in my hidden album. Whenever he told me that I was making things up, I would take myself back to the screenshots of his phone. Focusing on "reality on the ground".* Both emotionally and physically, I found myself pulling away. This distancing was a protective measure, a defense against further hurt, disappointment, and the risk of STDs. Despite my physical presence, my emotional bond with him was dissipating, especially given that he had shown himself to be untrustworthy. *You deserve better. You can do better. You are better alone. He is jeopardizing your health. He contributes nothing. The only thing that would change is you would have more money to spend on yourself. Why are you allowing this? Kick him the fuck out. He is trash. Stuff it down.* The question echoed relentlessly in my mind: *Why are you still with this asshole?* Conflicted emotions tore at my heart, creating a painful tug-of-war within me. One part of me yearned for liberation from the cycle of pain, drama, and betrayal that had become all too familiar. I longed for a life free from the clutches of whatever this was. Yet, another part of me clung desperately to the remnants of hope, believing that if I just tried a little harder, if I just worked a little more, things could be fixed. It was a battle between my rationality, which recognized the toxicity of the situation, and my emotional attachment, which still held onto the belief that love could conquer all. *I now recognize this struggle as a trauma bond, a deep emotional attachment formed between individuals due to repeated cycles of abuse, manipulation, and intermittent positive reinforcement. It can create feelings of loyalty or attachment to the perpetrator, despite the harm they've caused. Such bonds often make it challenging for the victim to leave or distance themselves from the relationship, even when they're aware of its toxicity.* As I grappled with my conflicting emotions, I recognized patterns linking my present relationship to my past dynamics with my father. The familiar threads of abuse and manipulation were all too evident. I came to the painful realization that my deep-rooted attachment and tolerance for such mistreatment stemmed not just from my current partner but from unresolved traumas in my past. *Oh God. Not that. Could it be? How is it possible? I spent my entire childhood chasing love, affection, acceptance, worth—everything from one man. This one man did everything in his power to shit on my love and never see me. And here I am. Chasing a piece of shit. A piece of shit who is thriving off of my unresolved childhood trauma. How is this possible? I thought I did the work. I did the work! I thought I was done with this. Clearly, I am not. Oh God. Growing up without my father's presence created a void that I subconsciously sought to fill in my romantic partnerships. It led me to unconsciously gravitate towards partners who mirrored the emotional unavailability and detachment I experienced from my father. Then I get sucked in and stuck to the cycle of the perpetual chase. I did do the work, but there is more. Okay, I want out, but I want to do it gracefully and amicably. Uncoupling. Gracefully. Always kind.* I started to pull away, and he sensed it.

The Setup

On what was meant to be a leisurely trip to his relative's house upstate, the promise of poolside relaxation quickly turned sour. The allure of the summer sun and the idea of tequila sodas seemed innocent enough, a simple way to unwind. However, as the day wore on, it became clear this wouldn't be the carefree outing I'd anticipated. As the drinks flowed, my perception became distorted, causing disorientation and a growing sense of detachment and dissociation. Time became fragmented, leaving me with sporadic memories and an overwhelming unease. Several hours, especially our journey home, felt like they had disappeared into a haze. Once we arrived home, he transformed. Rather than expressing concern for my well-being, he unleashed a torrent of anger, pinning all the blame on me. He berated me for what he saw as excessive drinking, using the situation to belittle me. His accusations weighed heavily on me, compounding my humiliation. And when tears filled my eyes, he labeled them as manipulative, further fueling his anger. I had trusted him to watch over me, to ensure my safety. But his response obliterated that trust. His reaction plunged me into doubt, wondering if maybe I had indeed overindulged and brought this on myself. However, I distinctly remembered having only four drinks—certainly not enough to lead to such a severe memory lapse, even under the sun. While I was aware of the concept of 'sun drunkenness,' I'd never experienced such a disorienting blackout. A chilling realization began to dawn on me. Over time, I discerned that his outburst was less about genuine concern for me and more a manipulative tactic. Deep down, something felt off. The dizziness, the lost hours—it seemed like more than just the effects of alcohol. A lingering fear suggested a darker, more sinister explanation than mere intoxication. The disorienting episode, the absent memories—it felt like an entity beyond my control had seized me. A chilling thought anchored itself: *he drugged you.* The offputting story he had once shared in jest about drugging a former girlfriend suddenly didn't seem so innocuous. Initially, I had dismissed it as a distasteful joke, a dark fabrication, but the grim reality now presented itself. *He had been revealing his true nature.* A horrific realization began to solidify—I had been drugged. These insidious whispers of drugging reverberated in my mind, suggesting the horrifying probability that I had been intentionally incapacitated for his advantage. Although the complete truth remained elusive, I couldn't disregard the gut feeling that the incident was far from ordinary. My drinking amount seemed reasonable to me. Could it have been the interplay of sun, heat, and alcohol? *Maybe.* But I had consumed alcohol under the sun before, more than today in fact, and never experienced dissociation or lost substantial chunks of time. It was as if I was trying to access missing pieces of a puzzle, but they simply weren't there. Suddenly, I snapped back to the present moment. My heart pounded, and adrenaline surged through me just in time to avoid the metal water bottle flying towards my head. As it crashed into the wall, leaving a clear dent, time seemed to decelerate. The mark it left was a disturbing reminder of the violence that had just occurred. I sat, frozen in shock and disbelief, unable to articulate the fear and betrayal coursing through me. His icy stare met mine, showing no remorse or comprehension of the severity of his actions. At that moment, I felt voiceless, the force of his aggression having stolen my capacity to respond. The room's atmosphere thickened with unspoken tension, as if the walls themselves were recoiling from the unleashed violence. He then added to the insult with a nonchalant dismissal of his violent act: "I didn't throw it at your head." The words echoed around the room, devoid of any real remorse or responsibility. He seemed to believe that this mere technicality would absolve him of his wrongdoing. I stood speechless, grappling with the reality that the person I had once trusted had morphed into a dangerous being with complete disregard for my well-being. This person was a stranger. That night, as I lay in bed, my mind spun with unanswered questions and troubling thoughts. The incident repeated in my mind, with every detail permanently etched in my memory. The disturbing possibility that he had spiked my drink, deliberately impairing my faculties and rendering me helpless, loomed over my thoughts. *Was it a pretext for his physical aggression, a way to rationalize and validate his violent outburst? Perhaps it was a calculated move to sow doubt and self-blame within me that he could later exploit, especially in front of his family, to undermine my credibility and consolidate his control.* The uncertainty and fear gnawed at me, eroding my sense of safety and trust. I found myself analyzing every interaction, and every gesture, searching for signs to either confirm or refute my suspicions.

Trigger Warning

The upcoming chapter contains explicit descriptions of physical violence and abuse. Reader discretion is strongly advised.

This chapter portrays graphic incidents of domestic violence, detailing an event where the protagonist is violently assaulted by their partner. It delves into the victim's subsequent emotional turmoil, encompassing shock, confusion, and self-blame, as well as the perilous cycle of minimizing and justifying the abuser's actions. Such content can be distressing, especially for those with personal experiences related to domestic abuse. If this subject matter might affect you, please consider your emotional well-being before proceeding. If you've faced trauma or are in a harmful situation, it's vital to reach out for support. Remember, you are not alone, and assistance is within reach.

Wake Up

On two separate occasions, he overstepped boundaries that should never have been breached, resorting to physical aggression by shoving my head forcefully into a wall. The first incident took place within the supposed safety of our own home, while his daughter was obliviously watching television in the next room. The second, during a vacation upstate, also occurred with his daughter mere rooms away. It felt as though he chose these moments strategically, fully aware that my desire to protect his child would keep me quiet. In both incidents, the pattern was strikingly similar. He would unleash his bottled-up anger, using venomous words to diminish and shame me. I can still recall the sensation of his hot breath and spit as he hissed threats in my face. Even in the face of his menacing behavior, I stood firm, refusing to back down. But my defiance only served to escalate matters. He'd corner me, pushing me back until I was pinned to the wall with no means of escape. Disregarding my safety entirely, he'd then thrust my head against the unyielding wall. He'd stand there afterward, almost expectantly, waiting for my response. His eyes, cold and dark, pierced into me, creating an aura of fear and intimidation. In the immediate aftermath, I was engulfed in shock and confusion, which clouded my ability to think and respond rationally. I minimized the gravity of his actions, convincing myself that these were isolated incidents of him momentarily losing control and that they would not repeat or escalate beyond the jarring collision of the wall and my head. But reflecting now, I grasp the extent of my misjudgment. By internally justifying his abusive behavior, I inadvertently signaled that his actions towards me were somehow tolerable. In doing so, I unknowingly validated and emboldened his violent tendencies. This was a severe lapse in judgment, and one I deeply regret, the burden of which I continue to bear. In dismissing his behavior as a momentary loss of control, I failed to acknowledge the deeper, underlying patterns of abuse emerging in our relationship.

Gifts

Amid the turbulence and abuse, there were interspersed moments of calm and normalcy. These brief periods, where everything seemed right, offered glimmers of hope, though they were fleeting and transient. They stood as poignant reminders of what our relationship once was, or what I had hoped it would become. In the aftermath of his heart attack, the fragility of life became starkly apparent, compelling me to deeply cherish and savor our moments together. It inspired me to plan a vacation to Turks and Caicos, despite his financial constraints. I hoped this escape would serve as a rejuvenating break, mending our strained bond. Throughout the trip, he exuded gratitude and warmth, momentarily dispelling the ever-present tension. Encouraged by seeing him genuinely at peace, I grew hopeful of reigniting the depth of our connection. With this renewed spirit, I orchestrated several trips to upstate New York, nurturing the belief that the love and goodness we once shared could be rediscovered. I took joy in spoiling us with lavish dinners at elite restaurants and surprising him with thoughtful gifts, from trendy sneakers to clothing. Every gesture was an expression of my determination to make the most of our time together, a response to the poignant reminder of life's unpredictability. When he seemed stressed about finances, I readily helped with car repair expenses. While these gestures stemmed from genuine affection and a desire to support our relationship, in retrospect, they often became entwined with the relationship's toxic dynamics. The fleeting moments of peace were consistently overshadowed by persistent abuse and manipulation. Despite my efforts to nurture a connection, the core issues remained unresolved, sustaining a relentless cycle of pain.

One day, as we prepared for our day, I casually broached the subject of children and expressed my excitement to become a mother someday. To my astonishment, he stated he no longer wanted children. This was a stark departure from our earlier shared dreams, plunging me into confusion and sorrow. I had held onto the vision of us starting a family together, believing he felt the same. However, his abrupt reversal forced me to face the reality that our futures might be misaligned. This moment marked the beginning of his unraveling facade. The truth, long obscured, became glaringly evident: I was now seeing a man who avoided genuine transparency. His refusal to acknowledge our prior talks about children was deeply hurtful. He even tried to discredit my recollections, implying the fault was mine with remarks like, "If that's what you understood, then something's wrong with you," a blatant attempt at gaslighting. *He told my sister, my best friends, and his daughters. Are they all crazy too?* I had a vivid recollection of our previous discussion. The clarity of our exchange left no room for ambiguity. Yet, his attempts to warp the reality and shirk accountability were deeply unsettling. These maneuvers started sowing seeds of doubt, making me question not just his words, but the foundation of our relationship itself. *Had he been deceiving me from the start? Did he derive some perverse pleasure from toying with my emotions?* The sudden change in our plans cast doubt on our shared history. Looking back, I recognized a troubling trend of manipulation. Gaslighting, a tactic he often employed, was designed to skew my perception of events. He consistently sought to undermine my confidence, muddle my thoughts, and keep me off balance. This insight drove home the painful truth that our relationship was built on a bedrock of mistruths and deception.

Consciousness

Many might wonder why I stayed so long without recognizing the signs of abuse. From the outside, it's easy to cast judgments and think, "I would never endure that." The reality, though, was more complex. I was oblivious to the growing toxicity, as behaviors that started as occasional outliers became the norm. This abuse often intermingled with what appeared and felt like genuine moments of affection, making it even harder to discern. His manipulation was insidious, with fleeting periods of kindness masking the overarching harm. Moreover, my childhood emotional wounds, specifically unresolved issues with my father, added depth to this quagmire. Subconsciously, I was chasing something from this relationship that had eluded me in my formative years. He tapped into this vulnerability, exploiting my past traumas to keep me ensnared. This not only made it tough to escape the cycle but also complicated my understanding of it. During moments of apparent peace, I'd convince myself that the turbulence was behind us. Yet, even in those times, a persistent unease nagged at me, suggesting something was fundamentally amiss. This constant internal tug-of-war left me entrenched in the cycle, feeling like I was caught in a rip tide, being pulled further and further away from the shore of clarity. I admit, I began this relationship from a position of deep insecurity and self-doubt. These feelings played a significant role in how I perceived and internalized his behavior. I harbored a belief that I deserved the mistreatment, viewing it as a manifestation of my inadequacies. Consequently, I often blamed myself, making it easier to accept and even expect the abuse. My need for his validation and approval, driven by my self-worth deficit, further entrapped me in the relationship. I hoped that his affection, however fleeting, would fill my internal void and confirm my value. This intense need for validation made me vulnerable to manipulation. By internalizing the blame for his behavior, I unknowingly perpetuated the cycle of abuse. Each episode not only eroded my self-esteem but also solidified my belief that I was undeserving of genuine love and respect. This became a self-reinforcing cycle, where every instance of abuse further entrenched my feelings of unworthiness. *You are not worthy. You are not enough. You are not lovable. They will never choose you.* I was deeply torn: one part of me believed in love and a brighter future, while another faced the undeniable reality of ongoing abuse. I held onto moments of affection, however infrequent, seeing in them glimpses of the person I had fallen for. These moments kept me anchored, fueling the hope that with patience, things might change for the better. Yet, even as hope glimmered, the signs of abuse became harder to ignore, starkly contrasting the tenderness with cycles of control and emotional upheaval. The weight of this truth grew heavier each day, making it clear that my hopes for change might remain unfulfilled. Confronted with this, my emotions ranged from denial to anger and sorrow. I wrestled with feelings of guilt, questioning my role in the dynamics, and whether my actions or inactions had somehow contributed to the abusive behavior. My understanding of the situation was clouded. I lacked the awareness to label my experiences as abuse. In my naiveté, I equated my enduring loyalty and efforts to please him with genuine love and commitment. I thought if I met his every expectation, I would secure his love and respect. *This is exactly what I spent my entire childhood doing. Becoming the perfect daughter so that my father would want me. Stand up straight, and smile. Don't ask for too much. Give everything, maybe then he will stay.* He was adept at targeting my deepest insecurities. Each demeaning comment and gesture was meticulously aimed at undermining my self-worth. With every encounter, he chipped away at my confidence, highlighting my perceived flaws. The persistent torrent of verbal abuse weakened my self-esteem, pulling me into a vortex of self-doubt. His words acted as a venom, leaving lasting emotional scars. Over time, his cruel narratives became my internal voice, leading me to question my value and doubt if I was deserving of genuine love and respect. He seemed to have sown seeds of self-doubt in me, which grew into an entangling web that muddled my identity. I was perpetually on edge, bracing for his next critique. Fear of his judgment kept me tiptoeing around him, desperate to avoid any trigger for his wrath. This ceaseless cycle was draining, blurring my understanding of my place in our relationship. Looking back, I recognize his manipulations were tailored to ensure his dominance. By making me doubt myself, he aimed to make me reliant on his validation. This suffocating dynamic ensnared me, eroding my self-worth. His conflicting displays of affection and mistreatment created deep cognitive dissonance, making it hard to reconcile his proclaimed love with the pain he inflicted. This turmoil clouded my judgment, anchoring me in hope and making me rationalize his behavior. I clung to the belief that love could prevail, thinking that if I just gave more, things would change. *Give more. Do more. Be better. Be more loving. Be more accepting. Give more.* Caught in a toxic dynamic, I grappled with confusion and self-doubt. His manipulations made me question my worth and sanity, clouding my judgment. Realizing the truth was challenging, but essential for reclaiming my identity. I recognized that his behavior stemmed from his deep-rooted insecurities, not my shortcomings. This understanding enabled me to shed the blame he placed on me, viewing our situation more objectively. I realized that I deserved better. His version of love demanded a sacrifice of my emotional well-being. True love should never come at the cost of one's self-worth or mental health. *You are a queen. Start acting like it. Wake up. Please. Please wake up.*

Change in Tides

Narcissists are known to reveal their true nature when they believe they have gained control and power in a relationship. As familiarity and trust develop, they become more comfortable displaying their abusive behavior. It is when a narcissist perceives their partner as dependent or less powerful that they may escalate their abusive tactics. Furthermore, if their needs are not met, they become increasingly overt in their manipulative behavior in order to regain control and assert their dominance.

There came a moment, a watershed of undeniable significance, though the exact timing of this profound transformation remains elusive. It was as if I were gradually emerging from a prolonged state of slumber, beginning to stir within a world that had subtly begun to alter around me. *Wake up. Wake up. Wake up.* This marked a distinct turning point in my life, a phase of awakening. I found myself amid an imperceptible change, the kind that happens so slowly and steadily that it's almost impossible to determine its exact inception. This was not an abrupt alteration, but rather a gradual evolution of circumstances, akin to the subtle change of seasons. *Wake up. Wake up. Yes. Rise.* As I awoke, the world seemed to shift along with my consciousness. It was as if the universe had sensed my awakening and was responding. Suddenly, the facade he had so meticulously crafted began to crumble, revealing an entirely different side of him, previously unseen. The once familiar gestures of kindness and consideration he used to offer started to fade until they became entirely extinct. What used to be a sense of comfortability had turned into an alarming sense of entitlement, and it seemed as though he was developing an unspoken claim of ownership over me. From nowhere, tempestuous arguments would spring forth, their intensity catching me off guard, like the unexpected roar of thunder from an otherwise clear sky. The aftermath was eerily akin to the wake of a fleeting summer storm. Once the turmoil passed, the sun would seemingly reappear, as if to deny the existence of the storm entirely. The aftermath was but shallow puddles that would soon evaporate, erasing any lingering evidence of the turmoil, save for the chilling memory etched in my mind. Gradually, the fragmented pieces of the jigsaw puzzle that was our relationship began to coalesce, offering a clear image that I had struggled to comprehend. The disjointed fragments of my experiences and observations were now aligning, illuminating a deeply unsettling pattern that had been camouflaged in our everyday interactions. The behaviors, the spoken words, the underhanded manipulations, and the more overt forms of abuse—they all began to form a disturbingly cohesive narrative of the reality I was ensnared in. As the fog of confusion and uncertainty began to lift, I gained a more profound understanding of the undercurrents shaping our relationship. The puzzle pieces, once jumbled and elusive, now found their rightful place, sketching a daunting picture of a truth I had been so reticent to acknowledge. Suddenly, the murkiness of the situation faded, replaced by a stark clarity that revealed the true nature of our twisted dynamic. *Am I going crazy? He is talking in circles again.* Caught in a relentless whirlwind of confusion and distress, I started questioning my sanity. His incessant monologues, the repetitive stories, spewed as if they were brand new, left me feeling lost. Any attempts to join the conversation were met with accusations of interruption, silencing my voice. I was served a word salad at every encounter. He argued against my every thought, not in a bid for understanding but for the thrill of disagreement, the sport of breaking me down. His need for control extended to policing my words, dictating my responses even in text messages. My attire, my physical appearance, everything was subject to his scrutiny. He'd condemn me for working out, yet he'd turn around to label me overweight. My personal space shrank further when he began to dictate where my phone should be while we drove. He'd escalate arguments on the highway, berating me throughout the journey, exploiting my lack of escape. His financial contributions dwindled over time, with a blatant sense of entitlement over my resources. Even simple things like sharing a ConEd bill triggered his ire. There was a jarring disconnect in his words and actions. His grand dreams for the future were never backed by concrete actions in the present. He was all talk with no tangible progress. He bulldozed through conversations, wielding an illusion of omnipotence, leaving no room for others' perspectives. Gradually, a realization dawned on me—I could do better. I deserved better. Why was I confining myself in a relationship that didn't serve my well-being? Was it even a relationship? I had missed nothing, it was just my failure to acknowledge the situation for what it was. I yearned for liberation. I realized that I was worth far more than this constant turmoil. But no, I couldn't suppress these feelings anymore. *I can do better. Yes. Yes, I can. I am better alone. What do I need to be in this relationship for? Fuck, this isn't a relationship. What is happening? What did I miss? Fuck, I didn't miss anything, I failed myself. I want out. I am better than all of this. Stuff it . . . fuck. I can't stuff this down. I am awake. Stop choosing this. Stop choosing this. Get out.* After the truth unveiled itself, I could no longer deny or ignore what I had always known deep down. I could feel that my vibrations were off, as if I wasn't supposed to be in my current timeline. The story of my life seemed stuck, like a skipping record, repeating the same patterns over and over again. I could hear the vinyl jumping, the cracks in the record becoming more evident than ever before. It was the first time I truly realized that my life was stuck in a loop, and I needed to find a way to break free and create a new narrative for myself. *This is not what I wanted. This is exactly what I said I didn't want. How did I get here? God, Kia, how did you get here? You are intelligent! You are successful! You are kind! You are good! How did you shrink into this small cage? How?* His systematic and calculated tactics blindsided me entirely. I was oblivious to his subtle yet relentless power drain, unaware that he was quietly siphoning away my vitality. While I was distracted, hunting for signs of sabotage in every direction but his, he sat there, smugly with a smile on his face, fully aware of the damage he was inflicting. He was the invisible hand pricking holes in my life vest, gradually eroding my resilience, all the while maintaining a façade of love and care. The malicious nature of his behavior soon became glaringly apparent. He relished the cunning strategy that would bring about my downfall, masking his intentions behind a façade of decency. Beneath the mask, however, was a predator driven by an insatiable desire for control. From the outset, I'm convinced that he had singled me out as his prey, skillfully identifying and cataloging my vulnerabilities with the precision of a predator, preparing for the perfect moment to exploit them. As the pandemic hit, plunging the world into disarray, he saw the perfect opportunity. He manipulated my virtues, my craving for tranquility, and my distaste for conflict, to ensnare me. He would orchestrate chaos from nothing, fully aware of how these tactics would disorient me. He took perverse delight in my ensuing struggle, his every move reflecting a chilling, Machiavellian calculation. His strategies grew bolder and more calculated with each passing day, his true nature becoming increasingly evident. With surgical precision, he manipulated every situation to his benefit, viewing me as his ultimate conquest, a trophy to be claimed. Our relationship began to feel more like a battleground, a place of relentless psychological warfare where every day brought new skirmishes. He knew exactly where to strike for maximum effect, turning my dislikes and preferences into weapons against me. It was only too late that I realized the extent of his surveillance, the microscopic attention he'd paid to my every move. He exploited the isolation brought about by the pandemic, twisting the societal need for distancing into a tool for manipulation. As someone who craved harmony and avoided conflict, I was woefully unprepared for his relentless onslaught. One of his preferred strategies was sleep deprivation. He would insist on keeping the television on at high volumes through the night, knowing full well it would disturb my rest. If I dared voice my discomfort, he would spin the narrative, accusing me of selfishness and inflexibility. Throughout the day, he would play videos on multiple devices, creating a harsh symphony of discordant noises. He claimed that this chaotic background noise was helpful to him, ignoring the anxiety and distress it caused me. Any attempt to reduce the noise would trigger his wrath, followed by belittling remarks about my inability to adapt. Each interaction with him was a strenuous uphill battle, and his responses when thwarted were akin to the petulant tantrums of a spoiled child. If his demands weren't met, he would plunge into sulking silence, isolating me as a form of punishment. This left me in an emotional limbo, humiliated, drained, and alone. His outbursts and the subsequent icy silence were weapons he wielded with precision, aimed at breaking my resolve and diminishing my self-esteem. As time passed, it became increasingly clear that his manipulative abilities were the result of years, if not decades, of honed practice. To my chagrin, I had unwittingly become his most significant project, a testament to his prowess in manipulation and control. He relished the power dynamic he had established, deriving a twisted sense of pleasure from my confusion, pain, and suffering. Simultaneously, he kept up an impressive façade for the world to see. He paraded himself as a man of wealth, intellect, and kindness, carefully curating this persona to maintain his image in society. I want to emphasize, however, that these attributes were mere illusions. He was not the affable, intelligent, and affluent individual he presented himself to be, but rather a skilled manipulator hiding behind a carefully crafted mask. His true character was marked by manipulation, deception, and a disturbing delight in others' distress.

Waves

As I gaze at the impending wave thundering toward me, an intense sense of inevitability and powerlessness consumes me. Regardless of my efforts, there's no eluding its imminent impact. The sheer force of the wave's energy feels overpowering, and I grapple to ready myself for the impending collision. Anxiety and fear take hold as I observe its menacing approach, the chilling realization settling in that I am on the brink of total immersion. Faced with this relentless force of nature, my options are limited—I am confined to bracing myself for the inevitable, alone.

Feeling the need to run.

Feeling like running nowhere fast.

Feeling lost.

Riding these waves, trying to hold on.

No lifeboat in sight.

I'm gonna float—not gonna drown.

Not gonna drown.

Whatever you do, keep focused on the light.

Not gonna drown.

Not gonna drown.

Not gonna drown.

The Reckoning

As fear and tension began to take root within me, I found myself trapped in a ceaseless state of apprehension. I felt as though I was treading on a minefield of eggshells, perpetually vigilant, constantly fearing that my actions or words might ignite his volatile temper. The burden of his wrath and the relentless emotional drain it caused became increasingly unbearable. In this suffocating atmosphere, I found myself losing touch with my identity. I began to suppress my needs and desires, burying them beneath the constant need to avoid conflict. My spirit dimmed as I prioritized maintaining a fragile peace over my well-being. Over time, this peace came at the high cost of my individuality, my emotions, and ultimately, my sense of self. I began to fade into the background, a specter in my own life, all in an effort to keep the peace in an environment where tranquility was a rarity. *Survival mode. You're gonna figure a way out. Just hang in there a little while longer. You can end this gracefully and peacefully. Endings are always hard but you always make it through. Conscious uncoupling. I am committed to being kind.* The visits to his father's house, once a sanctuary of warmth and connection, morphed into arenas of conflict. With every step across the threshold, I could feel a palpable shift in the air, a precursor to the simmering anger within him that was ready to boil over. It was as if his father's presence was a catalyst, stirring his wrath and making me an unfortunate target of his tirades. The presence of his father acts as kindling, igniting his smoldering rage. As we edge ever closer to the tipping point, I choose to keep my emotions veiled behind a carefully curated smile, offering minimal verbal responses. My movements are calculated and minimal, as if any sudden action could detonate the situation. I strive to be precise in my responses, curating each word, tone, and gesture with care, aiming to leave as little room as possible for misinterpretation or dispute. Every moment spent in that house was tainted with a sense of impending doom, a cocktail of tension and anxiety. I found myself on edge, waiting for the fuse to burn down to an inevitable explosion of rage. Departing from his father's house was an equally, if not more, horrifying experience. The tension within the confines of the car was almost tangible, a silent storm brewing. With bated breath, I braced myself for the imminent tempest. *Three, Two, One—detonation.* His piercing screams echoed in the confined space, hurling baseless accusations my way. He charged me with disrespecting him in front of his father, an incident fabricated in his volatile mind. He reproached me for being "too much," an indictment as vague as it was unjust. The harrowing journey home was marked by reckless swerving as he let his emotions commandeer the wheel. The steering wheel bore the brunt of his violent outbursts, serving as an unwilling outlet for his rage. The impact of each pounding reverberated through the car, further escalating the fear and tension. This ordeal was not just physically unsettling; it took a psychological toll as well, leaving me trembling in its aftermath. Fear had a stranglehold on my heart, its icy fingers leaving me in a state of perpetual dread, a helpless passenger in this tumultuous journey. This ordeal surpassed any road rage incident I had ever experienced. One particular instance still haunts me: In a moment of sheer terror and instinctual self-preservation, I found myself leaping from the still-moving car. It was as if his rampant fury had become a tangible entity, filling up the vehicle to the point where there was no room for me. His rage had pushed me out. Yet, he didn't let me escape the terror. He forced me back into the car, back into the heart of his wrath, prolonging the distressing experience. This was not merely an encounter with anger but an immersion into a terrifying world where rage dictated the rules. The car journeys home transformed into relentless reminders of his explosive temperament, signaling the unpredictable tempest that was to come. Existing in this unending state of apprehension and uncertainty wreaked havoc on my emotional well-being. As I contorted my identity in futile attempts to placate him and skirt around his fury, I could feel my sense of self gradually fragmenting. Yet, the more I strove to satisfy him, the more insatiable his demands grew. This left me feeling depleted and hollow, a shell of my former self. I found myself entangled in a destructive cycle, constantly sacrificing my mental and emotional health for the transitory tranquility of the moment. This was not just survival; it was a slow erosion of my identity, all under the weight of his ceaseless demands and explosive anger. In the treacherous landscape of this toxic relationship, even the simplest actions or utterances could be twisted and weaponized against me. I found myself in a continuous state of self-doubt, scrutinizing every movement and word I spoke, apprehensive that they might be misconstrued or seen as a pretext for his anger to erupt. My thoughts and emotions were dismissed, and invalidated, rendering me into a state of hypervigilance, perpetually on the lookout for strategies to circumvent his fury. In time, a painful truth crystallized in my understanding: his conduct did not mirror my deeds or reflect my value, but rather stemmed from his deep-seated demons. He deflected his internal rage onto me, positioning me as an effortless scapegoat for his combustible wrath. This pivotal understanding bestowed upon me a profound and transformative insight: I was not the source of the contentious issues, but instead a deliberate victim caught in his violent cycle of abuse. His actions and reactions were the outward manifestations of his deeply rooted rage, and I was surreptitiously compelled to bear the aftermath of his emotional tempest. In the face of his explosive wrath, I had been pushed into an unenviable role, taking the brunt of his storm while he remained the eye, calm and unperturbed. This epiphany marked a decisive turning point, serving as the extraction point from the relentless storm of his abuse. It was the critical crossroad where I made the conscious decision to start distancing myself, to begin separating my life from the persistent turmoil and pain he caused. *"I'm not going to drown. I'm not going to drown," I repeatedly told myself. "Just hold on a bit longer," I pleaded. A sudden realization startled me. "Wait. How long has this been going on? Has it been since the very beginning?" The truth hit me like a bolt of lightning. "What do you mean? Was it ALL manipulation?" As the horrifying reality unfolded, the pieces started to fit together. "Oh, it all makes sense now." I felt an overwhelming urge to escape, the urgency pounding in my veins. "Get out. Get out!" I screamed to myself. "GET OUT! GET OUT!" The declaration echoed within me, a loud rallying cry in my fight to reclaim my life.*

Trigger Warning

The upcoming chapter provides explicit descriptions of domestic violence, including physical assault and strangulation. Reader discretion is strongly advised.

This chapter contains graphic accounts of an abusive relationship, portraying verbal confrontations, explosive anger, and severe physical violence. Descriptions detail episodes where the protagonist is choked, pushed, and physically attacked, resulting in significant physical harm. The narrative sheds light on the relentless cycle of manipulation and abuse the protagonist endures, emphasizing their state of constant fear and defensive reactions during assaults. The content is intense and could be particularly triggering for those with personal experiences related to domestic abuse. Before proceeding, please consider your emotional well-being and personal boundaries. If you've faced trauma or are in a harmful situation, reaching out for support is vital. You are not alone, and help is at hand. Please prioritize your mental health and feel free to step back if the content is too distressing.

March 2, 2023 | The Purge

At dinner, I felt as though I were navigating a minefield with every word I uttered, and every action I took. A potent, unsettling undercurrent pervaded the atmosphere, distinctly different from other nights. It was as if his anger had taken on a life of its own, buzzing in the air like a live wire, its electric charge threatening to erupt at the slightest provocation. The oppressive weight of his imminent rage felt like a heavy shroud, suffocating my spirit, and squeezing the joy out of my existence. I could sense his underlying current of anger that seemed to crackle with electricity. Being in his presence was akin to balancing on a razor's edge, each moment fraught with the peril of potentially triggering his volatile temper. The facade of a healthy relationship was now stripped away, nothing but a fading memory, replaced by an agonizing pattern of baseless accusations, misplaced blame, and relentless verbal onslaughts. The anguish of enduring this treatment had etched a familiar, deep void in my heart. Returning home from dinner, the tension in the air transformed from a mere undercurrent into a tangible, stifling fog. With each step toward our abode, the foreboding sensation within me grew. It manifested as a visceral, sinking feeling deep in my stomach, gnawing at my sense of safety, eroding my fleeting hope for a peaceful end to the evening. The ominous silence of our journey was but the calm before the storm, a storm I knew was destined to break the moment we crossed the threshold into what was supposed to be our sanctuary. As we moved, his brisk pace seemed calculated, another ploy in his arsenal of control. His strides were determined, and unyielding, and I found myself struggling to match his speed. This subtle power play only further underscored my predicament—another litmus test I was doomed to fail, another strike against me in his unspoken tally. It was as if my inability to keep up was another point of contention, another "failing" for him to use against me, just one more thing I couldn't seem to do right in his eyes. As we ascended the staircase, I steeled myself for the tempest of anger I knew was on the brink of eruption. A torrent of unvoiced questions swirled within me, the loudest among them echoing with painful clarity: Why had he chosen me, when it seemed that he harbored such contempt for my very essence? His simmering resentment was a palpable force, a coiled spring poised to uncoil in a devastating release. Seeking a brief sanctuary, I hurried into the shower upon our arrival home. There, beneath the rhythmic patter of water droplets, I sought a transient reprieve, hoping the passing time might allow his boiling anger to subside, if only slightly. As I stepped out from the steam-laden sanctuary of the bathroom, a familiar sight caught my eye: his thumb and forefinger, locked in a slow, methodical dance. This habitual gesture, one that had become almost as familiar to me as the man himself, seemed to act as a barometer of his emotional state. With a sinking heart, I recognized it as an ominous portent of the storm that was yet to come. *Fuck. He did not calm down. He's been simmering. Breathe. Breathe.* This gesture of his was a chilling precursor, a harbinger that instantly put my body on high alert. Hastily, I dressed and positioned myself at the farthest end of the couch, gripping my water bottle as though it were a lifeline. *Inhale. One. Two. Three. Exhale. Breathe.* Again and again, I silently echoed this mantra, a futile attempt to calm the galloping rhythm of my heart and maintain my pretense of interest in the flickering television screen. I wrestled with the rising tide of fear and anxiety, clinging to the edge of my composure with white-knuckled determination. *Inhale. One. Two. Three. Exhale. Breathe. Inhale. One. Two. Three. Exhale. Breathe. Inhale. One. Two. Three. Exhale. Breathe.* Then, a comment slipped past my guard, an innocuous mention of a friend's recent return from a work trip in Singapore. It was but a harmless remark, a fleeting ripple on the surface of our strained silence. Yet, it was as though that ripple had disrupted a precarious balance. In an instant, his rage ignited, his voice booming out like a clap of thunder, reverberating ominously through the room. I felt myself shrinking, cowering beneath the intensity of his wrath. However, I couldn't let silence become my refuge anymore. Gathering every ounce of strength I had left, I rose to my feet and declared with a defiant firmness, "**Enough. This ends now. I'm done. We're over. I can't live like this anymore.**" My words lingered in the space between us, a proclamation of my intent to break free from the shackles that had bound me. The weight of this existence had become unbearable. Freedom, once a vague yearning, had become a burning need. Yet, my defiance seemed only to fan the flames of his anger. With each word of resistance I spoke, his rage burned hotter, transforming him into an incandescent embodiment of malice. He took a threatening step toward me, his hostility palpable. He shoved me with a force that rocked me off balance, but instinctively, I pushed back in an act of sheer survival. However, before I had the chance to react further, his hand was around my throat. His grip was vise-like, a cruel demonstration of his raw physical power fueled with rage. Each breath became a Herculean effort as his fingers tightened mercilessly, a dreadful crescendo of terror in this symphony of chaos. His grip grew tighter and tighter. In a desperate attempt, I fought to free myself from his vice-like grip. But within seconds, my back slammed against the solid leg of the couch, a brutal jolt of pain shooting up my spine. Before I could regain my bearings, he was upon me, pinning me to the floor, the pressure around my throat escalating with every passing second. His eyes, once familiar and even comforting, had now morphed into black pools of unrecognizable rage. His weight, all two hundred and twenty-five pounds of it, bore down on me, a monstrous presence that oppressed my very being. My attempts to scream were futile, the sound stifled by the pressure on my throat. The air in my lungs dwindled, replaced by an intense fear that gripped my very core. I was voiceless, defenseless, trapped beneath the heavy weight of his anger. I literally couldn't make a sound. *Oh*

God. Dear God. What is happening? Please, God. No. Please, God. Not this way. God, please. All my efforts to resist melted away, replaced by a cold, enveloping darkness. Consciousness began to slip away as the room faded to black. At some point, his iron grip slackened, and I felt the weight lift from my body. As he loomed over me, a figure of menace, I mustered every bit of energy left to cry out. But my voice betrayed me. A guttural whisper was all that escaped, barely audible, as if I were suspended in a haunting nightmare. *My throat. I can't speak. What's happening? What's happening?!* With a dizzying stumble, I clambered to my feet, my throat sore and raw. Almost instinctively, I lashed out, a primal urge of self-preservation propelling my right fist toward his face. The sharp connection momentarily surprised both of us. But his retaliation was swift and brutal. His fists came down like a torrent, a single blow so forceful that it rooted me to the spot, fear stealing my breath. Suddenly, he seized my right arm, punching me down to the floor. Instinctively, I curled up, my arms desperately attempting to protect my head from the incoming onslaught of his pummeling fist. But he didn't let go, he didn't stop, he continued his relentless assault. *One. Two. God. Three. Please. Four. God, please.* Eventually, he released my arm, his fury unabated unleashing his full rage. He towered over me, raining down blows with both fists. Pummeling my head. Each punch was a deafening thunderclap, full force, no mercy. Reduced to a defenseless heap, I could only endure. My ability to fight back was long gone, and my voice had deserted me. I was left helpless under the weight of his rage, every punch a crushing testament to my powerlessness. Standing over me, he pounded my head with both fists, using full rage. The sounds of my flesh on impact were in surround sound. *Is this real? How is this happening?* I just focused on counting the hits. *Five. Six. Seven. This is it. Everyone knows that I love them. Forgive me for my trespasses. Eight. Please. Stop. Enough.* The hits stopped. **Please. Stop. Enough.** was out loud. Each throb of my heart felt like a muffled drum in my chest, striving to escape the confines of my body. Desperately gasping for air, my body quaked with uncontrollable tremors. I gathered the strength to stumble into the bathroom, hoping to find refuge within its narrow walls. Confronting my reflection in the mirror, a wave of revulsion engulfed me. My battered body, the physical manifestation of the abuse, stared back at me with horrifying clarity. Pain screamed through every cell, manifesting itself visibly in my disfigured features. The grotesque swelling of my eye, a vicious reminder of the assault, bulged disturbingly. A violent shade of purple was already beginning to blossom on the left side of my face, accentuating the grotesque distortion. Crimson rivulets swirled within the white of my eye, turning it into a macabre tableau of the violence I had endured. Reality crashed into me with the weight of a freight train, making my breath hitch in my chest. My breathing turned shallow, and quick, my body spiraling into a state of hyperventilation that only amplified my sense of panic and despair. *This can't be real. How is this real? How could he do this? He is trying to kill me. Is this real? I don't know what to do. I need help. I need to be safe. I need help. How is this real? He's going to kill you. Be smart. He's going to kill you. This can't be real. How is this real? Oh God, I can't see. Oh God. Please no. This can't be real. How is this real?* He paced back and forth, repeatedly muttering 'fuck, fuck, fuck, fuck.' The echo of his restless pacing and the consistent string of curses filled the room. Gathering my remaining strength, I managed to fetch some ice and collapse back onto the couch, the chill of the pack doing little to ease the throbbing pain. The realization that I could no longer see from my left eye hit me like a bullet—a chilling thought that sent waves of panic through me. *Fuck I am blind. I can't fucking see. Calm down. Calm down. Be smart. Calm down. You must survive. Stuff it down. No emotions.* I forced myself to take deep breaths, reminding myself to stay calm, stay rational. Survival was paramount. I swallowed down the rising tide of emotions, remaining as emotionless as possible. The tremors coursing through me were a testament to the physical and emotional ordeal I had just endured. I could not stop my body from shaking. The room took on an eerie calm as he sat merely a foot away from me, his expression nonchalant. The accusation was stark, "Look at what you did." I was utterly dumbfounded, my mind struggling to reconcile the words he spoke with the reality of my physical condition. *No, No, No, NO. This can't be happening. What. What. No. This is not happening.* ***THIS IS REAL. WAKE UP.*** I snapped back, 'No. I don't know what you're trying to do, but YOU did this to me. YOUR fist caused this to my eye.' I reached for my phone and entered the password as quickly as my shaking hands would allow. He advanced towards me, looming over me, demanding, 'Who are you calling? Who are you texting? What are you doing? Each question landed like a punch, further intensifying my fear. His intimidating presence hovered above me. *Fuck. Fuck. Lock the phone. Throw the phone.* I threw the phone and said no one. He went back to pacing and shaking his head. *What should I do? Do I leave? But I am blind in my left eye. Maybe it's best to rest my left eye, as further stress can cause permanent damage. Oh God—what if it is permanent? Where do I go? Did the neighbors hear? When I went down was it loud? I can't remember. Are the police already on the way? No, it was too short and quiet. There is no way anyone is coming. No one is coming. No one is coming. You are in this alone, and you will get out of this alone. No one is coming. Don't die here. Survival mode. You must survive. For the love of self, stuff it down.* Seizing a fleeting moment of his distraction in the kitchen, I hastily retreated to the sanctuary of the bathroom. The sight that greeted me in the mirror was harrowing, but I knew it was important to document my injuries. Despite my trembling hands, I managed to take photos of my battered face. The very act of dialing 911 seemed an insurmountable task, the fear gripping me was far too overpowering. *What would he do if they came? He would know and then would he continue to beat me unconscious? He will kill me. Would anyone be safe? There are children in this building. I began to become overwhelmed.* I snapped more photos. You *must document this. If only for you.* I was scared for my life. *What is happening? Dear God, please don't let me be blind. You have to survive this. You* *have to play this fully until you can safely get out. Everything is going to be Okay. You are good. God, please. God, please. Kia, you are a good human. I love you. You will be safe.* In the silent depths of night, I lay trembling in bed, a stark contrast to his peaceful slumber, marked by rhythmic snores. His sleep came easily, an unconscious oblivion following his devastating rage. Meanwhile, I lay wide awake, gripped by an intense cocktail of fear and anxiety, my heart pounding a relentless tattoo against my ribs. The room was shrouded in a silence that seemed to echo my solitary distress. All I could hear were my shallow breaths, punctuated by the fervent whispers of my prayers.I found myself turning to my faith, seeking solace and protection in the divine. Each fervently uttered prayer to God, Archangel Michael, and Saint Lucia was a beacon of hope, a lifeline in the darkness that threatened to swallow me whole. I prayed for the restoration of my eyesight, both literally and metaphorically, holding onto the promise of a new dawn of healing and freedom. That night, sleep was a stranger. I lay vigilant amidst the turmoil of my reality, grappling with the profound uncertainty of my situation, clutching onto the delicate threads of hope. The dawn couldn't come soon enough.

No lifeboat in sight.

I'm gonna float—not gonna drown.

Not gonna drown.

Whatever you do, keep focused on the light.

Not gonna drown.

Not gonna drown.

Not gonna drown.

Get Out

He awoke with the dawn, the sky barely beginning to lighten, and began his usual morning routine for work. At 5:46 a.m., just before he left, he abruptly flicked on the light, casting a stark, unyielding glare onto my marred neck and distorted eye. I felt the weight of his gaze, filled with disdain, as he shook his head in silent disapproval. Then, without uttering a word, he left, the sound of the door closing echoing throughout the apartment. The moment the door clicked shut, a wave of calm washed over me, and the tremors that had held me in their grip slowly began to ease. Not wasting a moment, I reached out to some trusted friends in my life for help. I urgently needed medical attention for my injuries, and after that, to find the courage to voice the torment I had suffered. Thankfully, I was able to arrange an appointment with an eye specialist. The first step on my path towards healing had been taken. The scene that unfolded before the doctor mirrored something out of a movie: I was dressed in oversized sweats, hiding behind enormous sunglasses, my hands still trembling uncontrollably. I quickly concocted a story about being accidentally struck during a boxing class the previous night. However, the doctor's skepticism was evident in her questioning. "Did a loved one do this to you?" she asked, searching for the truth hidden beneath my facade. I mustered a smile while choking back tears and responded, "No, as I said, it was from boxing." But her professional instincts told her otherwise. She continued, "Your age, an emergency request first thing in the morning, and blunt force trauma. Are you sure this wasn't done by a loved one?" I was shaking. *They are going to call the police and hold you here. You have to beat him home. Sell it otherwise, you are finished. Get it together Kia.* Misunderstanding the gravity of the situation, I replied, "Umm, I understand. Can we just look at my left eye please, I am very sorry, I am scared for my eyesight." What followed in that examination room was a testament to the truth of the ordeal I had endured the previous evening. As the doctor attempted to administer eye drops, my reaction was visceral and uncontrollable. Fear surged through me, causing me to flinch and resist her efforts. I was unable to relax, forcing her to gently restrain me to complete the procedure. Throughout the process, I kept apologizing, expressing remorse for my uncharacteristic behavior. "I'm so sorry. This isn't like me at all. I truly apologize. This has never happened." The doctor, displaying remarkable compassion and understanding, was aware of the underlying truth. *How could she not be?* The news she delivered after her examination brought a mix of relief and concern. The blindness I had experienced was primarily due to swelling, which had begun to subside, allowing my vision to gradually return. Remarkably, my retina appeared to be intact. However, further follow-up visits were necessary to monitor my progress. She also wanted me to meet with a retina specialist. I assured her that I would comply with her instructions and be present for every appointment. With a renewed sense of urgency, I rushed home in an Uber, only to find him waiting, curious about my sudden absence. I informed him that I had visited an eye specialist, which perplexed him. "Why would you do such a thing?" he questioned with a hint of bewilderment. I looked him directly in the eyes and said, "Look at me. I was blind for the last twelve hours. I have to go back in two weeks." His response was a scoff, an attempt to undermine the specialist's expertise, insisting that her primary interest was monetary. This was a demon before me, acting as though nothing had transpired, as though my visit to the eye doctor was a trivial inconvenience. My resolve hardened. I would survive this. I had to. *He is acting as if nothing happened. Be calm. Steady. Be docile until you have a plan.* "I will always protect you," he said, but I couldn't breathe. "Kia, did you hear me?" I stood there, trembling. *Protect me? You almost fucking killed me. Play it cool. Play it cool. He has shown you that he is capable of anything, and the next time, he* ***will*** *kill you. God, there can't be a next time. Did he consciously choose not to kill me, or was I just lucky, or did God protect me?* I just looked at him, forced a smile, and walked away and I choked back vomit. He was so cold, his eyes empty and filled with darkness, but content with what he had achieved. He had gotten away with it. I was suffocating inside. My thoughts raced at breakneck speed as my eye throbbed, my throat hurt, and my entire face and head ached. I could feel where each one of his punches had landed, as if he had buried his rage with each hit. My voice still couldn't support a complete sentence or reach certain notes. He was here, walking around as if **nothing** happened, planning for the future. Asking me about making plans for my upcoming birthday, which is still two months away, it all felt surreal. *He is sick, and his behavior is sickening.* Every second, he monitored my movements, trapping me in an invisible cage. I had to be cautious, measuring twice and cutting once. There was no time to process my emotions or make sense of what had happened. I couldn't even fathom who this monster was, the one I had been lying next to for two and a half years. Sleep seemed elusive, a distant memory that I longed to reclaim. The trauma of the attack had left an indelible mark on my psyche, and the mere thought of closing my eyes filled me with unease. Nights turned into a never-ending cycle of restlessness and anxiety, as the images of that fateful moment replayed in my mind like a haunting reel. Over and over. Each night, I would lie there, my body elevated, my vision impaired by the blood edema in my eye, the pain still throbbing throughout my body. Sleep became an unattainable luxury, and the days stretched out before me, interminable and heavy with exhaustion and fresh with fear. As days turned into a seemingly endless nightmare, it became increasingly evident that he had no intention of leaving voluntarily. He clung to my life like a stubborn tick, relentlessly digging deeper under my skin, refusing to let go. Despite my direct and forceful conversations with him, urging him to leave without delay, the pressure he exerted on me only intensified. He dismissed my pleas, minimizing the gravity of the incident and invalidating my feelings with callous indifference. He seemed to derive a twisted satisfaction from the power he held over me, relishing in the control he had so ruthlessly seized. His behavior was no longer that of a loving partner but rather a cruel and sadistic tyrant. Each day, he subjected me to belittlement, trivializing my physical and emotional symptoms as if they were inconsequential. Even the simple act of refilling my ice to soothe my wounds was met with scoffs and disdain. Remorse seemed to be a foreign concept to him, a notion that had no place in his twisted mindset. To him, he had achieved his victory—complete and utter control over me. He reveled in his newfound power, relishing in dominating every aspect of my life. His actions were fueled by a sadistic pleasure derived from witnessing my gradual deterioration. He derived satisfaction from the constant intimidation, making sure I felt small and powerless in his presence. *I don't know how much longer I can endure this. I don't want to die here. This isn't my timeline. This isn't my timeline. This isn't my timeline. This isn't my timeline.* In my quest for a reprieve from the terror that held me in its merciless clutches, I found sanctuary within the austere confines of my gym's women's locker room. There, hidden from his oppressive gaze, I allowed myself to crumble, to surrender to the overwhelming emotions that I had been suppressing. Safely sequestered in an isolated corner of the room, I collapsed, my body sliding down the icy wall as though my strength had abandoned me. I sat there, a tragic figure, my trembling form huddled against the cold, hard tile. Each silent tear that trickled down my face was a testament to the unbearable torment that was my current reality. Each drop echoed my silent pleas for relief, for rescue, for release. During my breakdown, a woman appeared, her role at the gym defined by her cleaning supplies. She paused in her tasks, her gaze heavy with empathy and concern. Her eyes, though filled with compassion, held a profound sadness, a recognition of a pain she couldn't alleviate. It seemed as if she wanted to lend a comforting word or gesture, to express her sympathy in some tangible way. Yet, it was as though the words were trapped, held captive by an invisible barrier of uncertainty and awkwardness. In an attempt to alleviate her concern, I offered her a tremulous smile, a nonverbal assurance that I was aware of her presence, her sympathy. I gave a slight nod, an acknowledgment of her silent support. Although no words were exchanged, a powerful bond was formed at that moment. The exchange was brief, yet profound, a fleeting connection amidst the stark reality of my situation. I remained there, huddled in that corner, the echo of my silent tears a stark contrast to the bustling activity of the gym beyond. The cold tile offered a harsh comfort, a solid grounding amidst the turmoil of my life. In this secluded refuge, I allowed myself a moment to grieve, to feel, and with each passing moment, I felt myself diminishing, my spirit shrinking into a fraction of its former self. The words that yearned to escape my lips, to cry out for help, remained imprisoned within me, suffocated by the weight of the trauma. As I glimpsed my reflection in the mirror, the image staring back at me was a haunting sight. Bruises marred my face, silent testaments to the violence inflicted upon me. Bloodied and battered, my countenance mirrored the pain and anguish that words could not express. Tears continued to flow, tracing a path down cheeks stained with both physical and emotional wounds. In that moment, the person I once was seemed like a distant memory, replaced by a broken and fragmented version of myself. The mirror I gazed into served as more than just a reflector of my physical self; it was a portal into my soul, fractured by the relentless torment I had endured. It echoed back the silent screams of desperation and yearning for escape that had become my internal monologue. Every silent utterance that ricocheted within my mind—'**Please. Stop. Enough.**'—resounded with a haunting intensity, each syllable bearing the weight of my stifled cries. It felt as if a long-awaited train of comprehension had pulled into the station of my consciousness. Its arrival brought with it the stark realization that I could no longer tread this destructive path. A feeling of entrapment overcame me, a sense of being lost in a labyrinth with no discernable exit. My reality had become a daunting puzzle, each piece representing a step I needed to take to reclaim my life. Confronting my circumstances meant acknowledging the monumental challenge that loomed before me. It meant needing to legally and swiftly extricate him from my home and life. The prospect of navigating through the legal system, while also confronting the chilling fear of potential retaliation, shed light on the cruel reality many victims face when contemplating whether to break their silence or to continue bearing their suffering in silence. My quest for help and information was met with a deluge of contradicting details and a barrage of complex options. Each turn I took in this labyrinth of legalities felt like entering a new level of confusion and complexity. The information available was a complex mosaic of legalese and procedure, making the task of understanding and applying it to my predicament overwhelmingly difficult. It was an illuminating insight into the challenges that deter so many from pursuing justice. *Family court? Criminal court? Police reports, and medical records—do I need everything before I come forward? Do I need a lawyer? I need an order of protection—does a piece of paperwork? Is it too late to do anything?* The burden of navigating this legal maze was stifling, draining me both emotionally and physically. I found myself at a point where I could distinctly comprehend why so many victims elect to 'let it go,' attempting to move forward in their lives despite being submerged in a sea of pain and gasping on the harsh air of injustice. The journey towards seeking justice and protection is undeniably treacherous. It is a road not easily traveled, brimming with systemic obstacles, legal entanglements, and emotional landmines. Yet, amid these daunting challenges, this path is also lined with the indomitable courage and resilience of survivors who refuse to be hushed into oblivion. They stand as a testament to the strength of the human spirit, refusing to allow their voices to be lost in the whirlwind of institutionalized bureaucracy and societal prejudice. It was at this critical juncture that I realized the importance of my voice, and the significance of my narrative. My story carried a weight, an undeniable truth that held the potential to make a difference, to maybe even pave the way for others trapped in a similar cycle of fear and violence. The realization that my voice could resonate and inspire change gave me the strength I needed to continue down this complex road to justice.

Portal | Interlude

Gazing into the mirror, I found myself confronting a stranger. It was me, yet almost unrecognizable—my visage marred by grotesque bruises and an eye engorged with blood. Shame welled up within me, gnawing at the edges of my self-esteem. How did I end up here? How did I permit such monstrous brutality to violate my personhood? These physical reminders were not merely symbols of the physical torment I had suffered; they were the manifestation of deep-seated emotional traumas that would undoubtedly require more time to mend. I found myself teetering on the edge of an abyss of self-loathing, second-guessing my worth, scrutinizing my decisions, and challenging my capacity to ensure my safety. Yet, amidst this storm of self-doubt, a glimmer of resolute spirit began to flicker, slowly yet defiantly refusing to be snuffed out. I would not let this ordeal define me, I resolved. I would not let myself be relegated to the position of a helpless victim. With each new sunrise, I was grateful for life, for the chance to behold my reflection in the mirror, however disfigured, and acknowledge the woman staring back. This image served as a beacon of my resilience, my fortitude, and healing potential. I found myself whispering prayers for rejuvenation and renewal into the depths of my being. I yearned for the comforting cloak of normality, to stride into any space without carrying the visible emblems of my recent trauma. I looked forward to a time when my outward appearance was an accurate representation of the internal strength and grace that had weathered the storm. I longed for the day when my presence would resonate with vibrancy and life rather than the somber echoes of a soul savagely bruised. I made a conscious choice to wrap myself in a blanket of self-love, to envelop my spirit in warmth and kindness. I chose to unshackle myself from the unnecessary chains of shame and guilt, acknowledging that I was not defined by another's heinous acts. And, most importantly, I vowed to ensure that neither myself nor anyone else would ever inflict such pain upon me again.

Letter to Survivors

Dear Brave Soul,

I've just put down my pen from writing about raw and challenging episodes of domestic violence, and as my thoughts lingered on those lines, I couldn't help but think of you and others who've bravely faced their past. It takes immense courage to confront a narrative that mirrors painful memories, and I deeply admire your strength in doing so. It's never easy, and I want to hug you tightly and remind you that the weight of trauma you bear was never yours to carry. You deserve every droplet of love, every ounce of respect, and endless kindness.

Life sometimes feels like navigating a maze with its complex twists and turns of emotions. Know this—you're not wandering alone. Many of us are walking beside you, lending a hand, a listening ear, or simply our silent presence. I'm right here with you, as part of a compassionate community that genuinely wishes to see you thrive.

Reading about domestic violence can stir a storm inside. It's okay to feel, to hurt, to seek shelter until it passes. Lean on your loved ones. Reach out when you need to. Breathe, cry, and remember that healing is a journey, not a destination. Your experiences might have marked chapters in your story, but they don't define the entirety of your book. The courage with which you face each day, the hope you carry, the love you give—that's the real essence of you. With every dawn, there's an opportunity for a new beginning, and you, my friend, deserve the most beautiful ones.

Please cherish yourself. Laugh often, love deeply, and never forget your immense worth. Every scar you carry is a testament to battles faced and battles won. Keep shining, for your light guides many, perhaps more than you'll ever know. Remember, you're part of a vast tapestry of souls that stand with you, for you. You are truly cherished, and I believe in the brilliant future that awaits you.

With warmth and deep respect.

Hotlines:

National Domestic Violence Hotline: 800-799-7233
National Sexual Assault Hotline | 1-800-656-4673
Suicide and Crisis Lifeline | 988

Charges

The relentless question, "Why are you protecting him?" reverberated in the corners of my mind, a haunting echo that filled my days and nights. I felt trapped in a tempest of conflicting emotions, teetering on the edge of a precipice. I was not consciously sheltering him but rather yearning for an end to the torment, a refuge from the whirlwind of pain. I desired the dissolution of this nightmare, a chance for my wounds to heal, for life to regain some modicum of tranquility. The monumental decision to report the incident was like a leaden weight on my psyche. It cast long, dark shadows on my thoughts, and I couldn't evade the potential ramifications. *Would he be sentenced to prison? Would the revelation cost him his job, his means of survival? What about his daughters? How would they navigate the tumultuous sea of emotions if their father was incarcerated? And how would he cope with the harsh reality of prison life?* I struggled to envision him enduring such a circumstance. These questions besieged my mind, gnawing at my already damaged conscience. It felt like I was ensnared in a moral quandary, where each option seemed to offer its unique brand of suffering. Looking back, I comprehend a critical aspect: Throughout this storm of thoughts, there was a distinct absence of concern for my well-being. My focus was outward, revolving around the potential repercussions for him and his loved ones, rather than the healing and justice that I rightfully deserved. The reality of my situation did not fully manifest until a transformative conversation with my cousin. Her voice, threaded with a potent blend of concern and conviction, held a question that struck me like a lightning bolt, "Do you realize you could have died?" The severity of her words punctured my shields of denial, rendering me vulnerable. For the first time, I grappled with the true extent of the peril I had encountered—the delicate tightrope between existence and oblivion that I had unwittingly traversed. After ending the call, I echoed her question out loud to myself, "Do you realize you could have died?" In the solitude of my kitchen, I sank to my knees, overwhelmed by a torrent of uncontrollable sobs. The realization was painful, yet I couldn't, and didn't want to, halt the flood of tears. I had been ensnared in a cycle of survival, focusing solely on enduring each harrowing day. The daunting task of living through his periods at home, while devising a plan to expel him from my life, monopolized my thoughts. My immediate struggles clouded my vision, hindering me from seeing the broader scope of my predicament. It was as though I was lost in a vast, impenetrable forest, the towering trees blocking any glimpse of the world beyond. Consumed by my daily skirmishes, I failed to discern the road ahead or picture a life beyond mere survival. This claustrophobic wilderness became my reality, and I was blinded to its limits. Then came the chilling realization: *'You almost weren't here anymore.' Mom would've been left sifting through his lies, forced to swallow his version of the story. My essence, my very being, would've evaporated, leaving nothing but a fleeting memory for Mother and my sisters to mourn. How did it come to this? I saved him, believing in the sanctity of life, yet he almost tore me from this existence. At fifty, he's never once taken responsibility for his actions. Fuck him.* In the five agonizing days following the attack, he continuously trivialized and disregarded the enormity of the incident and the physical and emotional wreckage it had wrought on me. In his warped perspective, nothing significant had occurred, and I was merely a shattered mess, a product of my own making. His incessant gaslighting and manipulation were corrosive, warping my grasp of reality and my self-esteem. His behavior, from threateningly waving his hands inches from my injured face to changing his address to the home he was supposed to leave, served as constant reminders of his instability and sickness. The repercussions of the assault led to me having unpredictable bouts of crying, often finding solace on the cold, impersonal floor when my world seemed to be collapsing. In those moments of desolation, his stature appeared to inflate, his aura grew colder, more threatening. My tears seemed to fuel his dominance over me, his power seemingly magnifying with every tear I shed. Standing at this life-altering crossroads, it dawned on me that shielding him was not the solution. My worth extended far beyond the agony he had unleashed upon me. I was entitled to justice, healing, and the freedom to voice the atrocities he had committed against me. The decision to shatter the oppressive silence and fear gripping me marked a turning point. It meant welcoming the strength that resided within me and daring to stride toward a future where my voice reverberates, my suffering is recognized, and my spirit is liberated. He feasted on the scars of his past, parasitically thriving off his trauma. Around him, a ring of enablers fortified his warped worldview and nurtured his illusions, allowing him a grotesque freedom to inflict suffering upon others. It was amidst this darkness that a fundamental shift stirred within me, culminating in a crucial question that hung in the air, demanding resolution: "Why are you protecting him?" I grappled to find an answer. Surviving his abuse was merely one phase of my odyssey. I was keenly aware of the subsequent path I had to tread, fraught with physical and emotional aftershocks. The wounds he had etched into my being would serve as lingering reminders of the relentless trauma I had been subjected to. Beyond the physical and emotional toll, there was an additional weight to shoulder: the necessity to reveal this daunting truth to potential future partners. The brutality of the assault could not simply be swept under the rug, buried in the hopes of moving forward. He could not be left untouched, free to ensnare others in his destructive web. "Accountability" became my rallying cry, an anthem for justice. I felt an imperative duty to ensure that he faced the repercussions of his heinous actions, and that they were duly recorded to deter future harm. No other woman should have to endure his violent hands. The thought of another unsuspecting woman becoming his prey, her blood indirectly on my hands, was unbearable. I refused to allow that possibility to manifest. I resolutely decided not to pacify his family, who had voiced their relief when I initially chose to forgo police intervention. Their expression of gratitude rang hollow; my actions were not intended to shield their comfort or uphold their family facade. It wasn't about perpetuating their generational delusions either. My decision was centered on seeking justice, on insisting he face the repercussions of his brutal actions, and above all, it was about preempting further harm. There was no ulterior motive, no compromise on these principles.

A friend who lived a very similar storyline in the past came to my aid. She quickly connected me with a locksmith, and within thirty minutes, my locks were changed. She and her husband then arrived at my house to help me pack all of his possessions. Whatever containers we could lay hands on, trash bags sufficed. The plan was crystal clear: I would call him once his work hours were over and recite a prepared script: "The locks have been changed. Your belongings have been packed. My friends are here to help." The plan was not to ambush him.

Naturally, this news didn't sit well with him. He lost it, "What's gotten into you?" quickly spiraled into wild accusations of **me** having repeatedly hit him in the face. He dared to claim that I did to him what he did to me. It was as if my medical records meant nothing. *This is insanity. Insanity.* His claims were a jumble of irrational thoughts. His anger soon transformed into verbal threats, insisting that my friends had better be gone by the time he returned home. Moreover, he made it clear he had no intention of leaving and that I would have to 'learn to deal with it". Rage-filled calls punctuated our conversation, adding a cinematic touch to the whole drama. As his stall tactics continued, my friends had to leave for work. Seeking immediate support, I texted my sister who lived only a few blocks away, asking her to come over right away. The moment she stepped through my door, she was visibly shaking. Upon catching sight of my battered face, her confusion peaked. "What's going on?" she asked, to which I narrated the entire saga. Still trembling, she demanded we throw all his belongings out the window. I explained to her that we could not do that legally, and that I intended to continue to handle the situation with as much dignity and grace as possible. My phone rang, the display showing it was my mother. It seemed the time had finally come. As I answered and shared the ordeal with her, including his refusal to pick up his belongings, her response was firm and resolute: "I got this." Within minutes of hanging up, she called back to inform me that he would arrive by 8 p.m. with his father to collect his things. I marveled at her efficiency and ability to handle the situation—my mother truly is a saint. Apologies flowed from me to my mother and sisters for keeping them in the dark about the situation. I wished I could offer them more, but I was emotionally and physically drained. In less than half an hour, my mother was at my doorstep. The three of us—my mother, sister, and I—began the process of carrying his things down to the landing for his collection. Upon his arrival, he audaciously tried to argue his case with my mother, asking her, "Don't you want to hear my side?" It was shocking to imagine that he thought the mother of the woman he had physically beat would be interested in hearing his version of the story. With a calm demeanor and her innate strength, my mother rebutted, "No, men don't hit women. If it were up to me, you would be in jail. Collect your things and leave." His response was nothing short of childish, expressing concern over his TV: "What about my TV, who is going to take it down?" Amidst everything going on, it seemed a trivial worry, but it was all he seemed to care about, not the impending threat of jail or the severity of his actions. My mother calmly assured him that the TV would be professionally dismounted, and that he could schedule a time in the next couple of days for him to retrieve it from her. Without any further objection, he packed up his and his father's car with his belongings and left. My mother chose to stay with me that night, providing me with much-needed solace and strength. For the first time in six days, I was able to sleep. But peace was not yet my companion as I awoke at 2 a.m., breathless, with my heart pounding and stomach knotted as if my body was reliving the attack. But I allowed it, letting the tidal wave of anxiety wash over me, accepting it as a part of my healing journey. With his oppressive presence no longer haunting our shared space, I could finally breathe, think, and process my experiences free from his overshadowing influence. I started to comprehend the gravity of what I had endured—or rather, what I had triumphed over. Without the constant threat and stress, my body began to relax and re-regulate into a state it hadn't known in over two years. My body, pushed to its limits in survival mode, was finally allowed a reprieve. And for that, I owed it an apology. *Body, I am sorry. I love you.* To my soul as well, for the deep wounds inflicted and the healing that was yet to come, I felt the need to express my regret. *Soul, spirit of mine, I am so sorry. I love you.* Even in his absence, I found myself wrestling with the decision to file a police report. Calls for action resonated loudly from all around, yet amid this cacophony, I sought solitude. I needed a moment to gather my thoughts, to introspect, to discern my desires from the demands of others. It was essential for me to reflect deeply to fully understand the implications of my upcoming actions and ensure they weren't influenced by anything other than facts. The choice I was about to make was momentous, and I was acutely aware that it was I, and I alone, who would bear the weight of its outcome. Awakening on Thursday, a stark realization hit me: *He's hunting again.* Suddenly, the situation transcended my narrative. It wasn't merely about me anymore; it was about the next woman he might ensnare, and those before me who had stayed silent in their suffering at his fists. Galvanized by this thought, I contacted the police to file my report. As the grim details of my ordeal poured forth, I felt a sense of determination hardening within me. This was not merely recounting a traumatic past; it was an assertion of justice, a step towards shattering the stifling silence and holding him responsible for his heinous deeds. It was an avowal that I would not be muzzled any longer, and that my voice would resonate alongside the many survivors demanding justice and societal change. When the officer disclosed the charges, the gravity of the situation sunk in—it was all becoming terrifyingly real. The enormity of the event could no longer be downplayed or dismissed. I had survived a major ordeal. His machinations had painted our interaction as a mere heated argument, an attempt to distort the brutal reality of his actions. But seeing the charges inked on paper instilled a sense of validation. My ordeal was undeniable, not a product of overreaction or distorted perceptions. It underscored a stark truth: I survived. That affirmation echoed in my mind, growing stronger with each repetition. I survived. I survived. Above all, I was still alive.

Timeline of Events | 2023

March 2nd: Attack.

March 8th: Locks changed | Home reclaimed.

March 9th: Sat alone for the first time to make a clear decision.

March 10th: Filed a report with the NYPD.

March 11th: Warrant issued for his arrest. He requested time to turn himself in on April 17th to get his affairs in order. I found out about this date on March 30th and advocated for myself at the precinct. He was arrested on the evening of March 30th.

March 30th: His arrest. I was issued a Temporary Order of Protection.

Charges:

Class D Felony, Strangulation | PL 121.12 00
A Misdemeanor, Assault W/int Causes Phys Injury | PL 120.00 01
Violation, Harassment 2nd-Physical Contact | PL 240.26 01

April 14th: He filed a false report against me in retaliation (I was not aware at this time).

April 25th: My arrest warrant was issued. After hearing a rumor about it, I hired a private attorney who confirmed it.

May 2nd: Accompanied by my attorney, I turned myself into the NYPD. I was arrested and sent to Central Booking for arraignment. My court date was set for June 15th.

May 17th: His first court date—adjourned to July 27th.

May 31st: Call between my Attorney and the Assistant District Attorney.

June 15th: My court date—adjourned to August 11th. The 30/30 deadline is on August 2nd. The DA failed to file any paperwork or notes.

July 27th: His second court date—adjourned to October 12th.

August 11th: My final court date—all charges against me were vacated, dismissed, and sealed.

Facing the Waves of Trauma

Flashbacks are involuntary memories or vivid and distressing experiences of past abuse. They can be triggered by various stimuli, such as a sound, a smell, a touch, or a situation that reminds the survivor of the abuse they experienced. Flashbacks can feel like reliving the trauma, causing intense feelings of fear, anxiety, panic, and helplessness. They can also lead to physical symptoms such as sweating, shaking, and rapid heartbeat. Survivors may feel like they are losing control or going crazy during a flashback. Flashbacks are a common symptom of post-traumatic stress disorder (PTSD) and can have a significant impact on a survivor's daily life and functioning.

The drumming of my heart echoes the rhythm of my chaotic thoughts as I brace myself against the imminent wave of recollection, a force that seems relentless and unyielding. The questions assail me: *Will I withstand its impact? Can I stay afloat amidst this emotional tempest?* The wave crashes upon me with an overwhelming roar, overpowering my senses, its sheer ferocity sweeping me off my feet and dragging me into its turbulent depths. Feeling disoriented and unsteady, I grapple for stability, wrestling against the raging currents that threaten to pull me under. The water consumes me, its inexorable grasp propelling me in erratic directions, leaving me feeling exposed, overwhelmed, and vulnerable in the face of this uncontrollable tempest. In that disquieting moment, a profound realization dawns on me: surrendering to the wave, relinquishing any semblance of control, is my only recourse. Consciously, I adjust my focus, endeavoring to maintain an aura of calm and resilience, clinging tenaciously to the belief that I can steer my course through this tempestuous sea. I adapt, utilizing my instincts as a guiding compass amid the turmoil. It evolves into a battle for survival, where each passing moment elongates into an eternity. Drawing on every ounce of strength and resolve, I urge myself to ride out the stormy wave. Each breath becomes an affirmation of my perseverance, a testament to my unyielding spirit. Even as the struggle takes its toll, I refuse to succumb to the overwhelming forces threatening to envelop me. I clutch onto the glimmer of hope that burns within me, secure in the knowledge that I possess the resilience to withstand this storm. I remain unyielding, deriving comfort from the realization that, despite the formidable challenges, I am gradually regaining control as the relentless waves of PTSD begin to dissipate.

I had my back to the wave.

I heard the silence and felt the impact.

I was under.

Everything moved slowly.

There was no sound.

One arm stretched out reaching for help.

I felt myself being pulled further out so I pleaded in my mind.

Please. Stop. Enough.

I was choking on his rage.

The rage he could no longer swallow.

The rage he could no longer keep suppressed.

The rage that secretly kept me his slave.

I am done with his rage.

I have had enough.

I woke up on the shore.

It was over.

I felt where I took the hits.

I also felt free.

Free from the anchor inside me.

The wave had severed the tether.

Forever.

I am free.

Aftermath

In the wake of his permanent expulsion from my life, I found myself ensnared by the haunting specter of 2 a.m. panic attacks. Jolted awake from deep slumber, I gasped for air. My heart pounded in my chest, my stomach clenched with dread, and cold perspiration drenched my body. The echoes of trauma resonated deeply within me, challenging my very sense of self. In those moments, connecting with myself and seeking comfort felt as daunting as scaling a steep cliff. Time took on a disorienting quality, elongating into an intimidating expanse as I wrestled to reclaim control over my careening thoughts. With a trembling hand pressed against my chest, I initiated a purposeful dialogue with my inner self, guiding each breath with mindful intention. This act of mindful breathing became a sanctuary amidst the turmoil, a beacon guiding me toward regaining balance and control. Each inhalation was an affirmation of my existence, each exhalation a release of the anxiety that gripped me. The dialogue with myself—the rhythmic cadence of my breathing—served as an anchor, grounding me during these tumultuous episodes. *Inhale. Exhale. You are safe. You are protected. You are safe. I love you. You are loved.* The steady rhythm of deep, mindful breathing served as my steadfast anchor, a lifeline guiding me back to the comforting shores of the present moment. To augment this sense of grounding, I would twine my St. Michael chaplet around my wrist, the symbol of protection imbuing me with fortitude. As I did so, tranquility would gradually seep into my being, enabling me to surrender once more to slumber, buoyed by the reassurance of my safety. Yet, even the act of sleeping transformed into a formidable task, with my thoughts galloping untamed and my nervous system wrestling to recalibrate itself. I had overlooked the profound toll that stress and trauma had exacted upon my body. It was a poignant revelation, acknowledging the extreme conditions I had withstood—both preceding and after the traumatic episode—resting beside an individual who had come perilously close to extinguishing my existence. Then, there were the flashbacks. Once relegated to the realm of movie tropes, their chilling reality had insidiously permeated my existence. These unwelcome intruders would ambush me at unforeseen moments, hijacking my consciousness during moments of tranquility or distraction. With a jarring abruptness, I'd be catapulted back to the horrific scene of his towering figure, unleashing a storm of merciless blows on my helpless form. The unchecked violence, the explosive rage, the overwhelming sense of vulnerability as I folded into myself in a futile effort to evade the barrage—the nauseating echo of flesh against flesh still rang deafeningly in my ears. Fear, dense and asphyxiating, pulsed through my veins, commingling with the scorching pain and blinding terror. I felt frozen, ensnared by the ghoulish specters of my past. It was a plunge into the abyss of an interminable nightmare, where fear and panic twisted into an unforgiving stranglehold. Yet, amidst this chaotic tempest, I found an oasis of calm within my breath. Each inhale became a lifeline, pulling me away from the shadowy depths of my past, while every exhale released a fragment of the terror that clung to my being. With this rhythmic dance of breath, I began to navigate the turbulent waters of trauma, guided by an inner compass of resilience and hope. *Inhale, Exhale, One, Two, Three—again. You are safe.* I learned to tune into the rhythmic cadence of my breathing, using each purposeful inhale and exhale as an anchor to the present moment. Each breath served as a reaffirming whisper that I was safe, that I had freed myself from the suffocating clutches of abuse. Reestablishing this connection with myself, rooting myself firmly in the reality of the here and now, demanding a concerted effort on my part. Within this turbulent tempest of memories, I needed to find a tranquil harbor, a place of calm. There were instances when I noticed myself unconsciously holding my breath, a reflexive response from my body seeking to insulate itself from the visceral anguish embedded within those haunting echoes. These vivid flashbacks, interspersed with unsettling periods of dissociation, exerted a formidable toll on my psyche, leaving me feeling emotionally drained and vulnerable. To help manage these overwhelming surges, I sought solace in Eye Movement Desensitization and Reprocessing (EMDR) therapy, a therapeutic technique that served as a beacon guiding me toward a sense of grounding and internal equilibrium. During this healing journey, it became imperative for me to nurture patience and self-compassion, to treat myself gently while navigating through the residual layers of trauma. I soon recognized the critical need to not bear this burden alone and reached out to my trusted network of family and friends for support. Their comforting presence and empathetic understanding served as my lifeline, providing a wellspring of strength during my most vulnerable moments. I remain deeply grateful for their unwavering solidarity, a testament to the transformative power of collective support in the healing process.

The Shore of Myself

Flying monkeys' refer to people who support the abuser and assist in their manipulation or control of the victim. The term originates from the 'Wizard of Oz' story, in which the Wicked Witch of the West dispatches her army of flying monkeys to do her bidding. Similarly, in abusive relationships, the abuser may enlist friends, family members, or acquaintances to execute their abusive tactics, such as spreading rumors, intimidating the victim, or even physically threatening them. These 'flying monkeys' may carry out the abuser's orders willingly or might be unwittingly manipulated by the abuser's lies and skewed accounts of events.

I sought refuge in the serene expanses of Astoria Park, drawn to the tranquil murmur of the flowing water. There, in a quiet corner, pen poised over paper, I plunged into the ocean of my memories from the past two and a half years. What drove me was not sorrow or nostalgia, but an unwavering resolve to dissect each moment, to untangle the complex tapestry of events that had led me to my current circumstances. I was on a quest to comprehend the hows and whys of everything that had transpired. I knew there had been warning signs, subtle hints that eluded my awareness at the time, nothing that explicitly signposted the violent turbulence that lay ahead. But in retrospect, I realized there must have been signs. His propensity for violence was too second nature, the way he gave free rein to his fury, too practiced. It was not a novice's act; he had trodden this path before, repeatedly. I was at least his third victim, a realization that dawned on me as I discovered the identities of two others who had suffered at his hands. I left no stone unturned in my introspective journey, scrutinizing the overlooked signs, the crossed boundaries, and the violated personal spaces. Each of these elements, once disregarded or rationalized, now came under my relentless examination. Determined, I endeavored to shed light on the truths obscured by skillful deceit, unmasking the lies that had been artfully dressed as reality. The unraveling of his fabricated reality left me staggered. His alleged service in the Coast Guard was a sham, a striking revelation that made me question the veracity of every detail he'd shared about his life. His extensive criminal history, filled with violent transgressions, was a shocking discovery, though not entirely surprising given my experiences. Even more disturbing was the realization that he had betrayed his family and friends on multiple occasions, throwing them under the bus to evade taking responsibility for his egregious actions. His willingness to sacrifice those around him to protect his image revealed the depth of his deceit and lack of integrity. Each new revelation further unveiled the extent of his deception, making me feel as though I was navigating through a labyrinth of lies. The man I thought I knew was a mere phantom, a figment of his manipulative storytelling. I realized I had known nothing of his true identity, and the more I delved into the truth, the more I was taken aback. Immersing myself in understanding the psychological dynamics at play, I endeavored to unravel the motives and rationale behind such appalling behavior. I meticulously examined every aspect, desperate to glean some semblance of sense from the bewildering complexity that constituted his actions and choices. Furthermore, I committed to exposing the roles of those who had been unwitting, or perhaps even complicit, accomplices in his grotesque masquerade. Recognizing them, I hoped, would shed light on the wider systemic issues that enabled such behavior and abuse to persist. This intricate exploration was not just about holding him accountable, but also about understanding the societal constructs and individual failures that had facilitated his destructive path. Coming to terms with the fact that his family, or at the very least, the majority of them, were privy to both his past and present actions, yet chose to remain silent, was both baffling and deeply unsettling. Their silent complicity not only shielded him from facing the consequences of his actions, but also facilitated his continuing cycle of abuse. Their silence posed a haunting question: how could they knowingly expose others to such danger? Even though I am an adult capable of making my own decisions, I couldn't help but feel that there should have been a moral responsibility to share certain critical information. If I had known that someone posed a danger, I would undoubtedly have spoken up. Their silence makes them complicit in his actions. I grappled with their collective lack of integrity, trying to make sense of their refusal to expose the dangerous reality that they were well aware of. Their silence raised a painful question: How many more would suffer as a result of their complicity? After delving into the depths of the madness I had escaped from, I came to a chilling understanding: The relationship I had with him was nothing more than an illusion. Every moment, every shared memory was part of a carefully crafted plan, a facade designed to give him control. I was unknowingly a piece in his manipulative game, trapped in a reality that was never genuine. I discovered that he would fabricate a pseudo-reality, uttering lines borrowed from TV sitcoms and movies. This artifice, carefully constructed, was a part of his manipulation tactics, further blurring the line between reality and his deceitful narrative. My emotions, sincere, heartfelt at the time, were elicited by this artificial reality, akin to the feelings evoked when we watch a movie. I might have cried, laughed, or felt joy, but the cause, I now realized, was fabricated. Reflecting on the experience, I recognized that there were only two potential outcomes in that situation: one was to live my life trapped in his convoluted version of reality, forever subjected to his whims of rage and control. The other, even more dreadful possibility was losing my life altogether. Now that I had escaped, I was determined to rebuild my life on my terms, free from abuse and toxicity. My journey of self-love and healing initiated the transformation of my environment. Reclaiming my space was the first significant step. With the assistance of a friend skilled in spiritual cleansing and blessing rituals, I purged my surroundings of his residual energy and any tangible reminders of him. The cleansing was both empowering and therapeutic. The act of purging was instrumental in eliminating potential triggers, effectively making my home a haven once again. My healing process was not linear; it was punctuated with setbacks and victories alike. There were periods of progress where the burden of trauma seemed to lighten, and others where I felt ensnared in a perpetual state of anxiety. Through all these fluctuations, I exercised patience, granting myself the necessary time and space for recovery. Self-care was an essential part of my healing journey, with an emphasis on my physical, emotional, and mental well-being. I practiced self-compassion, absolving myself from any perceived failures or shortcomings, understanding that they were part of my human experience. The waves of trauma, though persistent, were losing their intensity over time. Emotional processing was crucial in my journey of recovery. I permitted myself to grieve, to cry, and to let go of the emotional burden that came with the abuse. Suppressing these emotions was not an option; instead, I allowed myself to experience and express them freely. Each tear shed was a testament to my strength, a sign of healthy processing. "*You are safe forever,*" I would remind myself, "*I love you.*"

Retaliation

Retaliation within the context of abuse is a deeply unsettling mechanism, designed to amplify the abuser's control and dominance. It typically manifests as a deliberate, malicious reaction whenever a victim seeks protection or assistance. At its core, the goal of such retaliation is to embed fear, ensuring that the abuser remains in control and that the victim remains hesitant about attempting to break free. When retaliation takes a physical form, it often signals an escalation in violence, where the abuser intensifies their attacks to punish any perceived defiance. These violent episodes can range from brutal beatings to life-threatening actions, all meant to deepen the victim's sense of entrapment and make them think twice about standing up to the abuser in the future. However, retaliation isn't limited to physical acts alone. Abusers may resort to tactics like filing false police reports or making unfounded allegations, all in a bid to tarnish the victim's reputation and credibility. Such actions can critically hamper the victim's prospects of seeking help or justice through legal channels. By weaving a web of deceit and half-truths, the abuser further tightens their hold, amplifying the victim's feelings of vulnerability and isolation. Upon taking legal measures to remove him from my life, his control over me was curtailed. The intimidation methods he once used, like menacing calls and messages, were blocked thanks to the order of protection. However, six weeks later, he retaliated by falsely accusing me in a police report, attempting to coerce me into dropping my legitimate charges against him. This retaliation prompted a shocking revelation: his extensive, violent criminal past, laden with gun-related offenses. Discovering that I wasn't his first victim not only intensified my pain but fortified my determination. My heart went out to others who had silently suffered his tyranny. What left me staggered was his audacious claim that I'd threatened him with something that looked like it could have been a pistol, especially considering his history with firearms. When he assaulted me, throttling my neck and pummeling my face to the extent that I lost sight in my left eye, at which point did this imaginary threat arise? I was immobilized, huddled defensively, taking the blows until he deemed it enough. His adeptness at exploiting the justice system to dodge repercussions was evident. He found refuge with his family, who shielded him despite knowing his deeds. How could they, especially with daughters of their own, support someone with such violent tendencies towards women? Whether rationalizing his behavior as a result of past traumas or arguing that it wasn't their place to step in, their complacency made them equally guilty in my eyes. Their silence is only bolstered by a legal system that seems flawed, allowing chronic abusers to misuse the very platform meant for protection. Internally, I grappled with a truth: Had I simply let him be, he'd have likely preyed on another unsuspecting soul. While part of me yearned to move forward, my innate sense of justice pulled me back. I couldn't ignore this stark reality. His reprisal filled me with trepidation. He'd strategized, betting on my crumbling under the weight of his false allegations. The potential impact on my professional standing and future loomed large in my mind. It was agonizing to think his baseless claims might tarnish the reputation I'd painstakingly built. His lengths to further harm me, to exploit stereotypes and lie, underscored his depravity. He aimed to weaponize racial and gender stereotypes, casting me as the "angry black woman" in his twisted narrative—a tactic I was informed he would employ. This calculated strategy was a deliberate attempt to undermine my credibility, further highlighting his manipulative nature. Yet, I remain unyielding in my determination to not let his false portrayal define me. Being black and a woman is not synonymous with anger. My heritage—a rich mosaic of culture, combined with resilience forged from navigating a world rife with discrimination—instills in me profound dignity. The bravery of my ancestors, who battled for justice and equality, empowers me. Yes, I recognize the unique challenges black women face, as do all women. But I am not consumed by anger. Instead, I channel this awareness towards positive action, championing empowerment, equality, and understanding. My voice emerges not from bitterness but from a drive for justice, empathy, and a brighter future for women of all backgrounds. By confronting the abuse I faced head-on and in public, I am breaking free from imposed narratives. I am not a simple stereotype. I am a complex individual with a gamut of emotions, aspirations, and dreams. I stand firm in challenging and dismantling damaging stereotypes that diminish the experiences of women everywhere. In me is the embodiment of love, strength, and transformative change. No attempt to misconstrue my identity can waver my core beliefs or determination. I personify strength, grit, and unwavering resolve. His deceit cannot overshadow the truth of who I am. While he anticipated an explosive response, he encountered an eloquent silence. Even as fear whispered its doubts, I drew strength from my innate resilience and the unwavering support of loved ones who knew the truth. I stood firm, certain that truth would reveal his manipulations. I refused to let his actions define me or deter my quest for justice and healing. I've discerned a disturbing flaw in the justice system: its vulnerability to exploitation through vindictive false accusations. It's concerning that arrest warrants can be swiftly issued without comprehensive investigation, often treating the accused as guilty before a thorough examination of the facts. This practice not only undermines the principle of presumed innocence but also erodes trust in the system. The fact that someone can jeopardize another's reputation and freedom using false claims, without proper scrutiny, highlights a significant lapse where fairness should prevail. We must champion reforms demanding meticulous investigations to safeguard the rights of the accused. Every claim, especially retaliatory false accusations, requires rigorous scrutiny. To renew confidence in our justice system, it must unwaveringly uphold fairness and due process. If I had acted as accused, I would've owned up to it. Guided by a deep belief in accountability and extreme ownership, I confessed to punching him retaliating in self-defense after he strangled me, fully prepared for any consequences. With an intrinsic respect for truth and integrity, I grapple with his blatant disregard for human decency. His deceitful claims aim to intimidate me into abandoning my charges against him. However, I will not waver from the truth. His attempts to distort reality cannot change the facts. I am resolute in refusing to bear the weight of potential future victims. Knowledge of his history of violence, coupled with an understanding of the silent torment many endure fearing retaliation, fuels my determination. Whenever anger surfaces, I view it as an opportunity for growth, knowing that all challenges are transient. I garner strength from the legacies of my ancestors and find comfort in standing with truth and justice, anchored in the belief that righteousness will ultimately triumph.

Day 122

On the 2nd of May, my mother accompanied me to the 114 precinct on Astoria Boulevard South. I decided to don my favorite black, sleeveless, floor-length Theory dress, a deliberate choice to make a statement about who I was. With composure and dignity, I greeted the officers on duty, "Good morning, I am here to turn myself in." A palpable silence permeated the station, as if everyone present was holding their breath, waiting for me to burst into laughter and declare that it was a prank. After thanking my mother, I handed her my phone and reassured her that we would reconvene at Central Booking for my arraignment. The officers demonstrated kindness, choosing to not handcuff me until after my mother had departed. With poise, I accepted the cuffs and was led to my cell for processing. Before being escorted to the cell, I was guided into the main area where officers called out "Live" as a signal for all present that their body cams were active. I was then posed a series of questions—if I had children left alone at home, to which I responded, 'No Ma'am'; if I required any medical attention, again, 'No Ma'am'; and if I had any possessions on me, to which I indicated two item—twenty dollars in cash and my NYS drivers license, both tucked into my left boot at the knee. I was then led to my cell. I chose to treat my time in custody that day as an experiential lesson. It offered me a front-row seat into the inner workings of the system. I questioned how I could advocate for women effectively without having undergone the process myself. Therefore, I embraced the experience as an enlightening opportunity. I carefully observed body language, interactions, and the general conduct of the environment around me. I noted with interest how the police treated everyone with a measure of dignity and respect. Standing within the confines of the cell, I absorbed my surroundings—the disquieting blood stains on the walls, and the discomforting bench. Yet, through it all, I could see and feel the outside air whenever the station's back door opened. *See you're safe. You're good.* Time seemed to slip away. I only knew that I turned myself in at 7 a.m. Then followed the process—fingerprinting, a mugshot, lunch. I waited patiently as the arresting officer completed the necessary paperwork. *About 100 pages, I was told.* There were murmurs about transporting "the prisoners" to Central Booking. I caught the word 'prisoners,' which felt inappropriate, considering no one had yet asked me about my alleged actions. *Relax, this is a process. You are Kia, you are not a prisoner.* Observing the line of male detainees shackled together, I felt a surge of relief as I was kept apart. Among them was a man who emitted a discomforting aura, especially when I found myself close to him. Soon, we were herded into a van destined for Central Booking in Queens. Sensing the elapsed time but unsure of the hour, I respectfully asked the officers for the current time. Upon learning that it was already 2:25 p.m., I was struck by the substantial passage of time, more than I had perceived. In the van, I overheard the police radios—the channel was surprisingly quiet. Curiosity led me to ask the officers if the channel was exclusive to the 114th precinct or spanned all of Queens. I learned it was solely for the 114th. *Another fun fact learned. Keep your mind focused on the present.* As the van coursed down the highway, I found myself awkwardly positioned sideways in my seat to accommodate the biting handcuffs. Cars zipped past us, their occupants blissfully unaware of my predicament. A wave of melancholy washed over me, not solely for myself, but for others who might share this unfortunate circumstance but not have the support and love that I was fortunate to have. As I stepped out of the van, chills coursed through me. The atmosphere within Central Booking was starkly different, creating an unsettling shift so intense that it heightened the discomfort from the handcuffs around my wrists. I found myself chained to a bench as male detainees were led to a holding cell. Glancing at my wrists, I observed the raw, red marks from the cuffs, a glaring testament to my current reality. While I sensed the end of this ordeal was near, I also recalled tales of Central Bookings' infamously drawn-out process. Regardless, I steeled myself, ready for the extended wait ahead. When it was my turn to be processed, I was instructed to remove my boots and declare any money in my possession. After claiming my twenty dollars, I received a voucher verifying the amount. Once I had put my boots back on, I was directed to pose for another mugshot. I didn't understand the necessity but recognized it wasn't the time for questions. Following this, I was escorted deeper into the facility for a health screening. Most of this consisted of questions from a fatigued nurse whose voice was muffled by her mask. Despite the minor communication barrier, I confirmed my good health and expressed gratitude for her thoroughness. Finally, I was led to a cell where a lone woman sat. I quietly took a seat, absorbing the stark reality of my environment. The cells in this facility differed significantly from the precinct holding cell. The intersecting horizontal and vertical bars of the cell were dizzying to stare at for extended periods, making me feel somewhat disoriented. Contrary to my initial expectations, the cell was reasonably clean, devoid of any blood stains on the walls. However, the exposed toilet, lacking both privacy and comfort, served as a stark reminder of my present circumstances. Feeling a sudden wave of lightheadedness, I took a deep breath, trying to keep my composure. I approached the woman in the cell with me, gently asking if she was open to conversation. I mentioned that talking might help distract and ground me in this unfamiliar and unnerving setting. Usually, in moments of stress, I'd find solace in a call to my mother, a comfort clearly out of reach here. She kindly obliged. Being a mother herself, she began sharing her journey. As we exchanged stories, hers highlighted the troubling ease with which one can get caught in the justice system and, even more concerning, the immense challenge of navigating one's way out. It was a poignant reminder of the harsh reality many face: that the wheels of justice can sometimes feel like a perpetual cycle of entrapment. Before being moved to another cell, a new inmate was ushered into ours. Distressed, she voiced her story of abuse, and revealed, to our shock, that her abuser was in the adjacent cell. Her raw account resonated with my experiences. To cope with the rising emotions this triggered, I used EMDR techniques for stabilization. I crossed my arms and rhythmically tapped my shoulders, a gesture intended to anchor me to the present moment and distance me from the recent trauma. When I was transferred to what turned out to be my last cell of the day, it seemed almost like divine intervention. It was only through my inquiries that I could ascertain the nature of this move, as the system primarily functions on a need-to-know basis, leaving detainees mostly uninformed. To gain a clearer understanding, I introduced myself to the officers. "Hello, my name is Kia," I began, "This is all new to me. Could you please explain where I'm being taken next? Thank you, ma'am." In this smaller space, I found myself with another woman, in her predicament. Our interaction was short-lived. Alone again, my attention was drawn to the carvings and scribbles on the cell walls. I contemplated their origins, the stories behind them, and the potential consequences of their creation. Soon after, my attorney arrived. She asked how I was, "I've certainly had better days," I admitted with a half-smile, "but this isn't my worst." I light-heartedly mentioned that it seemed almost fitting for a domestic violence victim to process trauma in such a place, leading to a shared, albeit tense, laugh between us. She then presented a startling proposal from the prosecutor: to drop all charges from both parties during the arraignment. I was taken aback by the audacity of such a suggestion. The apparent disregard for thorough investigation and professionalism was alarming. To think that after enduring such violence and spending an entire day wrongly incarcerated, I'd simply acquiesce was beyond belief. The system had underestimated my resolve. Not long after my conversation with the attorney, an officer handed me a face mask—an odd accessory at this point—and then guided me to the courtroom. The gravity of the moment washed over me as I stood before the judge, the one who would decide my immediate future. Amidst the murmur of voices and the steady rhythm of courtroom procedures, my eyes instinctively searched for a familiar face in the sea of strangers. And there she was, my rock and pillar of strength, my mother. Seated towards the back of the room, she projected a calming presence amid the unfamiliar chaos. Despite the physical distance between us, her unwavering support was palpable, grounding me as I braced myself for the impending proceedings. As I stood in the courtroom, time seemed to dilate, accelerating and yet decelerating simultaneously. The scene was not unlike a movie—a frenzied flurry of activity under harsh lights, yet somehow muted, as though drained of vibrancy. The charges against me were read aloud, and my attorney promptly entered a plea of 'not guilty' on my behalf. The judge then issued a protection order in his favor. The absurdity of it struck me with its sheer incongruity. I was released. And just like that, it was over. I embraced my mother, the familiar warmth of her hug anchoring me amidst the whirlwind of emotions. I expressed my gratitude to my attorney for her tenacity and commitment, and we left the courthouse, our spirits worn but unbroken. Throughout the twelve-hour ordeal of my incarceration—a consequence of unfounded accusations—I felt like a condemned criminal, charged with a crime that simply never happened. Facing overwhelming adversity, I chose resilience over despair. Drawing from an inner reservoir of strength, I navigated this challenging chapter of my life with unexpected grace and composure. While fear and uncertainty loomed, threatening to consume me, I maintained balance and clarity. My resolve stood firm, a beacon of light amidst the storm. During those intense twelve hours, I experienced an awakening, discovering an innate strength and resilience previously hidden from me. This shift from fear to empowerment marked a pivotal transformation. In my interactions with the women I met, their personal stories deepened my commitment to advocating for women's rights. Each had a story etched on her face, leaving an indelible mark on my memory. My hope remains that they have found freedom in their lives. Upon reflection, I felt immense pride in how I weathered the ordeal, staying true to myself and emerging fortified. This experience stands as a testament to the enduring power of courage and perseverance in my life. Upon regaining my freedom, I faced the immediate and profound implications of the unfounded allegations against me. The fallout threatened my access to vital programs, jeopardizing my Global Entry and my previously unblemished record. It was astounding how swiftly these consequences materialized without a thorough investigation into the allegations. The weight of this miscarriage of justice, intensified by the prosecutor's apparent misuse of power, weighed on me daily. Yet, an inner conviction reminded me of my undeniable innocence, offering solace with the belief that everything would eventually be set right.

30-30

On the 15th of June, I arrived at court, accompanied by my mother and sister. There was an unexpected calm in the atmosphere that echoed the tranquility I felt within myself. The courthouse, with its stringent security measures, was reminiscent of airport checks. We navigated through security and found ourselves in front of screens, scanning for the designated courtroom for my case. Upon finding it, we settled outside, awaiting my lawyer's arrival. My attorney soon joined us, and after exchanging brief pleasantries, we entered the courtroom. The interior was much as I had expected—adorned with wood paneling, with rows of antiquated wooden pews providing seating. The room was bustling, filled with people engrossed in their discussions. It wasn't long before my name was called out, and I made my way to the front, flanked by my lawyer. However, when the judge requested the case documents from the District Attorney's office, it became starkly evident that they were ill-prepared. They appeared flustered, bereft of any pertinent documents, notes, or concrete information about my case. I was taken aback by this blatant display of disarray and lack of professionalism. The judge, noticeably irked, still granted them a few moments to regroup. Yet, they returned only to confess their unreadiness. Consequently, my next court date was rescheduled to the 11th of August. The inefficiency displayed by the District Attorney's office was disappointing, to say the least. Intriguingly, the scheduled date sparked my interest as it fell well beyond my 90-day window, which was due to expire on August 2nd. For those unacquainted with the process, when the highest level charge is classified as an "A" misdemeanor, the prosecution is obligated to present their case within 90 days from the date of arraignment—in my case, this took place on May 2nd. Failure to do so by this deadline results in the dismissal of charges and the sealing of all related records. The lack of preparedness on the part of the District Attorney's office was revealing—perhaps they found his narrative lacking in credibility. Were they attempting to avoid the effort of paperwork by postponing the proceedings? It baffled me how this system could be so lacking in consideration for individuals like myself—victims of violent crimes. When would it be my turn to move on? The right to a speedy trial hinges on two crucial principles. Firstly, it seeks to reduce the strain on the defendant by offering a defined timeline, thereby lessening the psychological stress and uncertainty that come with ongoing legal proceedings. The assurance of a resolution, irrespective of its nature, provides some emotional respite. Secondly, this right is anchored in the critical societal interest of promptly dispensing justice. Delays in case proceedings can erode public confidence in the legal apparatus and consequently decrease respect for the law. The swift resolution of cases is integral to maintaining the justice system's integrity and public trust. Delays in justice can foster skepticism about the fairness and efficacy of the legal process. By ensuring the right to a speedy trial, these underlying principles aim to balance the protection of the accused's rights and the preservation of the public's faith in the criminal justice system. Even though I yearned for immediate closure, I found comfort in the knowledge that the allegations against me were false. I had no reason to fret over any new developments between the present and the forthcoming court date. Parting ways with my attorney, I was enveloped in a sense of gratitude and confidence. Knowing that there was a definitive endpoint offered solace, signaling an imminent end to this exhausting and wasteful ordeal, for both the state and myself.

Summer Days

During the waiting period before the final court decision, I sought solace in healing and personal growth. The summer became a canvas of exploration, filled with journeys to new destinations and deepened bonds with those I hold dear. Each travel experience was more than just a geographical shift; it symbolized the vastness of life beyond challenges. In the company of cherished friends and family, their unwavering support shone even brighter. Every shared moment of laughter and connection reaffirmed my sense of self-worth and grounded me further. I used this time as a sanctuary for introspection and self-love, intentionally keeping shadows of negativity at bay. In their place, gratitude flourished. Recognizing the strength and resilience that carried me through the darkest times, I felt compelled to celebrate those who illuminated my path. By spending time with them, I not only expressed my appreciation but also deepened our ties, ensuring they knew their pivotal role in my healing. Each day was a step forward, a moment to relish the small victories that marked my progress. Whether it was finding peace in a tranquil location or sharing an intimate conversation with someone close, I welcomed every instance that drew me closer to recovery. There's an unmatched freedom in living in the moment, unburdened by past or future. Being fully present, and absorbing the world's beauty and intricacies, I was consistently filled with a deep-seated joy. Each experience served as a reminder of life's wonders, underscoring the restorative power of being present and embracing the journey.

August 11, 2023

While waiting in the courtroom for the judge to enter, my eyes wandered upward, landing on an inscription I hadn't noticed during my previous visit: "In God We Trust." It felt like a reassuring message from beyond, letting me know everything would turn out alright. The last time I was here, uncertainty had consumed me. Today, a sense of calm anchored me. As we took our seats upon entering, I overheard the District Attorney mention "30/30" to my lawyer. I recognized the term and its implications, allowing a sigh of relief to escape my lips. Their previous unexpected actions still fresh in my memory heightened my anticipation. As other cases were called out, their narratives momentarily intersected with mine. I sat still, letting the room's atmosphere wash over me, silently extending my gratitude and well-wishes to others present. The moment I had been waiting for was drawing near. My name and case number resonated through the courtroom. The judge began proceedings, and immediately, the DA moved to dismiss the charges against me. In response, the judge dismissed the charges, vacated the undue order of protection against me, and ordered all related records to be sealed. Turning to me, he declared, "Miss Lee, this is now over." Relief surged within me, revealing itself in a broad smile. Overwhelmed with gratitude, I placed my hands over my heart, then brought them together, bowing slightly and whispering "Thank you." The weight I had felt lifted, leaving me feeling buoyant and liberated. My mother and I celebrated with a tight embrace, our joy palpable, as if it could be felt far beyond the room. Subsequently, we proceeded to the clerk's office. After making a payment, I was handed two copies of my Certificate of Disposition. While one was for official retention, I planned to frame the other, placing it alongside my BFA. It would stand as a testament to my journey and the resilience it symbolized through this trying chapter.

Forgiveness of Self

The journey toward forgiveness is intricate, placing a profound emotional strain on my mind. Among the myriad feelings that engulf me, the ones I harbor towards myself weigh me down the most. I'm filled with regret for not seeking help from my support network earlier and for maintaining a silence about my reality. This silent struggle, which momentarily strained some friendships due to my inability to see the truth, compounds my emotional weight. I grapple with feelings of shame, pain, embarrassment, and the notion of wasted time. These emotions push me towards a deeper understanding of myself and a commitment to healing. In my therapeutic journey, I am reminded of an essential truth: I am not to blame for the ordeal I endured. Sometimes, doubt gnaws at me. I question how I can be blameless when I entered the relationship, overlooked red flags, and bore the abuse until it became physical. Yet, it's becoming clear that the onus is on the abuser, who chose to harm me. While many praise my strength, it's important to understand that there are moments when I don't desire strength but yearn for safety and peace. To forgive means to dissect my experiences, to understand the myriad factors that enabled the abuse, without taking on the blame for another's choices. In therapy and deep reflection, I am striving to shed the heavy mantle of self-blame that I've donned for too long. I am coming to terms with the undeniable fact that I am worthy of empathy, comprehension, and recovery. This path is not just about moving forward; it's about reasserting my inherent worth and reminding myself that I deserve love, respect, and dignity. As a survivor, I often find myself lost in a whirlpool of questions, draining my emotional reserves and leaving me unsettled.

But with each step, I'm seeking clarity and reclaiming my peace. Yet, amid these tribulations, I am committed to unearthing my inner strength and resilience, patiently untangling the complexities of my experiences, and steadfastly journeying toward the sanctuary of self-forgiveness and healing. How did I manage to overlook such glaring warning signs? Why did I compromise my core values, entrapping myself in a destructive relationship? What compelled me to stay, despite the escalating harm? How could I have been blind to the glaring reality that something was profoundly amiss? Why did I suppress my instincts, the internal sirens that were urgently clamoring for my attention? How could I have allowed someone to erode my boundaries, steadily whittling them down until nearly nothing remained? Why did I reject glaring realities, treating them as mere distortions of the truth? I find myself caught in a cycle of ceaseless questioning and introspection, fervently trying to understand how I permitted such a catastrophic situation to manifest in my life. I grapple with a torrent of self-directed inquiries, each one chipping away at my understanding of the past, as I strive to piece together a coherent narrative from the fragments of my experiences. Despite the complexity and pain of these questions, I recognize them as necessary steps on my journey toward healing and self-forgiveness. Navigating the path to self-forgiveness requires confronting challenging questions about the dynamics that bound me to an abusive relationship. I delve deep into the factors that made me vulnerable and perpetuated the cycles of abuse. Recognizing the power imbalances, manipulation, and coercion present is essential. Through introspection, I aim to understand myself, my experiences, and the societal influences that shaped my perceptions. Self-forgiveness is about recognizing these intricate dynamics and cultivating self-compassion. Despite my self-awareness, these questions continue to haunt me, fueling self-doubt. Reconciling the image of my empowered self with the memory of a fearful, battered version becomes an immense challenge. This discord is central to my healing, pushing me to understand patterns that once made me prioritize others over myself. I'm committed to unraveling the maze of emotions, past experiences, and learned behaviors that guided my choices. This journey involves deep self-examination, compelling me to confront my past and the times I endured mistreatment. Gradually, I'm addressing the emotional trauma that has left significant scars, both physical and mental. I challenge long-held beliefs, motivated by fear, that directed my decisions. In doing so, I stress the importance of self-compassion, and understanding that my past has shaped me, but it doesn't define me. Committed to confronting the truth, I face each challenge head-on, realizing that navigating these emotional terrains is essential for my growth and liberation. I know healing isn't a linear process, but in the toughest moments, the foundation for profound transformation is laid. Evading self-reflection now would only lead to recurring challenges, so I'm determined to break these cycles. Embracing the discomfort, I take solace in the fact that each step, no matter how tiny, brings me closer to healing, empowerment, and a future free from the shadows of my past.

Understanding

During my journey of self-discovery, enhanced by daily meditation and prayer, I delved into the depths of my inner self. This exploration unearthed suppressed questions and demanded a raw confrontation with my true essence. To my dismay, I discovered that I had subconsciously convinced myself that I was unworthy of love and that my desires mattered little. Grappling with this startling realization, a flood of suppressed emotions surged within me. I committed to facing these emotions head-on, navigating through the storm of fear, anxiety, anger, and resentment. I honored each emotion, giving it space without repression. This encounter with raw vulnerability taught me that these emotions were transient; they wouldn't define or overpower me forever. As they ebbed, moments of peace began to emerge, allowing me to reconnect with my authentic self. On this path, fraught with doubts and uncertainties, I am learning the art of self-compassion, forgiving myself for past vulnerabilities and choices that once seemed perplexing. I am coming to realize that abuse doesn't reflect my worth or intelligence but is instead a result of the abuser's twisted mindset and harmful behaviors. Gaining these insights, I now understand that healing isn't a linear process, but a winding journey marked by introspection and acceptance. Self-forgiveness doesn't occur overnight; it's a transformative process requiring deep understanding and self-compassion. It demands patience to unravel the layers of guilt and self-blame that reside within me. As I journey forward, I focus on offering kindness and empathy to myself, acknowledging my innate worthiness of forgiveness. Each step allows me to better embrace my experiences and foster a space where self-forgiveness flourishes. Through this ongoing journey, I am breaking free from past burdens and embracing renewed self-acceptance and love.

The biggest Why

"Why didn't I just leave?" This question echoed relentlessly within me, creating a storm of self-doubt. Though I saw myself as strong, intelligent, and independent, I couldn't reconcile why I stayed. This unspoken question was mirrored in the eyes of those who cared for me, with even the most compassionate loved ones trying to understand the complexities binding me to an abusive relationship. Their hesitancy to voice this out loud highlighted their caution against victim-blaming, so the question lingered, waiting for introspection. My desire for clarity was overwhelming. I sought to understand my choices against the backdrop of my self-image. The simple, yet shattering realization was that I didn't recognize the abuse until its most brutal manifestation—when he loomed over me, rage-filled, struggling me and then pummeling my head and face with his fists. Before this, my understanding of abuse was limited. Many of us primarily identify abuse as physical, often overlooking its verbal, emotional, and psychological facets. The profound deceit and manipulation someone can employ, even when declaring love, was something I hadn't fully comprehended. The idea that someone meant to protect me could also be a source of violence was unthinkable. After the assault, a flood of suppressed memories emerged, revealing that the abuse had persisted for over two and a half years. With this new insight, previously overlooked warning signs in our relationship became strikingly clear. I had either chosen to see the best in my partner or didn't want to confront the unsettling reality, so I dismissed these early indicators. Whether from hope for change or a belief that love could overcome anything, I minimized their significance. Who would've imagined that such subtle signs could foreshadow a devastating turn of events? It's essential to realize that abusive relationships don't develop overnight. They unfold subtly, eroding personal boundaries and altering perceptions. Those initial red flags, though seeming trivial in isolation, can pave the way for an escalating cycle of abuse. They hint at underlying power imbalances, often hidden beneath a facade of affection and charm. Reflecting on this, I recognize the human tendency, including my own, to hope and believe in the potential for change. This optimism can sometimes obscure the reality before us. Accepting that I, like many, succumbed to this vulnerability is part of my healing. My journey isn't about blame or regret but understanding human complexities and how we navigate relationships. Another aspect is influenced by narratives rooted in my childhood. The persistent internal narrative told me: *You are unlovable. You are undeserving. You are not enough.* This belief manifested outwardly, acting as a beacon attracting those looking to exploit it. My abuser was no exception. He wasn't extraordinarily manipulative or unique but a typical example. His expertise wasn't in intelligence but in identifying and targeting women with histories of abuse. Such predators excel at spotting vulnerabilities and use them to exert control. This pattern is sadly common among abusers. They prey on their victims' past traumas, using them for power and control. It's a sobering thought that if it wasn't him, another might have taken advantage of my vulnerabilities. It's worth noting that just as someone could have exploited my vulnerabilities, another might have brought joy and healing into my life. Importantly, recognizing these dynamics doesn't justify or excuse my abuser's actions. It's about understanding my personal history and its impact on my choices, not absolving the abuser of their misdeeds. My quest for insight requires delving into the childhood traumas I faced and their influence on my relationships. The pattern of seeking love and validation from my father, later mirrored in my relationship with my abuser, underscores the deep-rooted effects of my early years. As a child, I constantly sought my father's love and validation. But my attempts were often met with neglect or indifference, imprinting a pattern of seeking love from those unwilling or unable to provide it. This deep-seated yearning influenced my perception of love and my worthiness. In my relationship with my abuser, these dynamics resurfaced. I found myself recreating a familiar pattern of neglect and mistreatment, continually searching for love and validation, hoping for a different outcome. It's not uncommon for people to be drawn to what they know, even if it harms them. My subconscious convinced me that by attaining the love and approval I once sought from my father, I could heal past wounds. Yet, reality was far from this idealized notion. Recognizing this reveals the myriad emotions and psychological factors anchoring me in the abusive relationship. Ingrained narratives, fueled by self-doubt and fear, clouded my judgment, preventing me from seeing reality and hindering my ability to leave. Exiting such a relationship isn't just about deciding to leave. It involves unraveling deep emotional, psychological, and for some, financial ties that connect the victim to the abuser. One must face embedded shame, blame oneself less, and muster great courage for safety and recovery. Recognizing this complexity fosters understanding, challenges misconceptions, and aids survivors. This underscores the importance of empathy and compassion towards survivors of abuse and highlights that seeking help is both a sign of strength and a step toward freedom. Every survivor's journey is unique, and seeking help should carry no shame. I'm determined to highlight the intricacies of abuse and break the often oppressive silence surrounding it. Silence only perpetuates the pain and allows abuse to continue. Sharing personal experiences, especially about challenging subjects like abuse, is honorable. Genuine allies will offer unwavering support during vulnerable times, never wanting you to suffer in silence. Turning to trusted individuals, whether friends, family, or professionals, provides a pathway out of abuse and a start to the healing process. Speaking out is a powerful act that reshapes societal norms, fostering an environment where survivors are heard, believed, and supported. Let's bravely share our stories, dismantle stigma, and ensure survivors feel understood and comforted. By breaking this silence, we promote empathy and awareness, advocating for a society that stands firmly against abuse and prioritizes resources for healing. Let's work towards a world where survivors feel seen, their voices are elevated, and they consistently receive compassion and assistance as they build a brighter future.

The Gift

During a pivotal therapy session, a powerful realization emerged casting a beacon of truth amid the darkness of my experiences: my spirit remained unbroken. Despite enduring abuse, the core of who I am stayed untouched, reflecting my steadfast commitment to authenticity and truth. Throughout this ordeal, my core values—love, kindness, empathy, and compassion—remained unswayed. Amid the chaos, my inner resilience acted as a beacon, reminding me that my self-worth wasn't defined by external abuse. I never let that darkness snuff out my inner light. Tenaciously, I held on to my dreams, my aspirations, and the person I desired to be, defying the grip of darkness that loomed. This profound realization flooded my heart with deep gratitude and respect for the resilient spirit dwelling within me. Reflecting on my journey, it's evident: that my inner strength is immeasurable, guiding me through the toughest times and preserving my integrity. The radiance from within me is unfaltering, regardless of external circumstances. I stand as a beacon of resilience, embodying the unyielding spirit that resides in all of us. This symbol of courage and commitment to my growth propels me forward. I embrace life's challenges, seeing them as avenues for further self-discovery and evolution. My spirit guides me towards healing and transformation—a constant, luminous force. It assures me of my capability to craft a life filled with purpose and joy. I cherish my internal flame, recognizing its power and warmth. It's a continuous source of inspiration and strength, reminding me of my worthiness for love and life's blessings. My spirit anchors me, offering resilience and direction.

I Rise

Standing at the cusp of self-discovery, a sense of serenity envelops me, mirroring the tranquil waves that meet the shore. I move forward powered by courage, grace, and love, confident in my ability to shape the life I deserve. Through this journey, I've shed the weight of false beliefs, embracing profound truths about my worth. I've come to recognize that everything I've sought—love, compassion, kindness, strength, resilience—is innate within me. This understanding anchors me: I am complete and enough as I am. Fueled by a deep well of self-love, I navigate life's intricacies with assurance. Free from the need for external validation, I derive strength from the reservoir of love inside me. Every step reinforces my trust in my capabilities and the boundless potential to manifest my aspirations. By embracing my authentic self, I take charge of my destiny, rooted in my inherent value and energized by self-love. I'm profoundly grateful for the lessons, the resilience acquired, and the steadfast love I hold. With every moment, I cherish my existence, fully aware that I am worthy of love, joy, and all of life's gifts. As I enter my 38th year, I've found peace in embracing my flaws and cherishing my entirety. I've realized that healing doesn't mean erasing our flaws or chasing an unattainable perfection. Instead, it's about recognizing our imperfections as integral parts of who we are and loving ourselves fully despite them. True healing lies in accepting our authentic selves, with both strengths and weaknesses. My adversities have underscored the importance of trusting my intuition, viewing it as a steadfast guide through life's intricacies. Fear no longer holds me captive; I stand courageously, ready to embrace life's richness and unpredictability. Confidence radiates from me, rooted in a deep understanding of my resilience and authenticity. This clarity has liberated me from doubt and insecurity, empowering me to live purposefully and chase my dreams without bounds. My journey to fully love and trust others has been transformative. I've come to recognize my boundless worth and that I deserve all the joy and kindness life offers. I am a testament to my wholeness, asserting that I am deserving of love and joy. Free from self-doubt, my heart beats with freedom, and I cherish each moment of this incredible journey of life. The future holds endless possibilities, and with optimism and profound gratitude, I eagerly anticipate the wonders that lie ahead. *I am free, I am whole, and I cherish every step of this extraordinary journey.*

The Journey

When I first put pen to paper, I intended to explore the intricacies of my relationship with my father. As the narrative took shape, it became evident that my experiences transcended a mere father-daughter bond, encompassing universal themes of trauma, healing, and evolution. This journey of self-expression taught me that many silently bear burdens similar to mine. I felt compelled to break this silence, to offer both solace and a beacon for those grappling with their challenges. Sharing such personal revelations requires utmost sensitivity and empathy. Yet, it was essential to create a space where others could recognize that together, we possess the strength to surmount adversity. My narrative, woven with threads of vulnerability, resilience, and hope, became more than just a quest for personal healing. It underscored the profound impact of authentic storytelling—its capacity to connect hearts, challenge societal norms, and herald transformative change. I hope that by revealing my journey, I might inspire others to reclaim their narratives, thereby redefining their destinies. Writing this memoir was both a cathartic process and a deep dive into understanding my identity and resilience. It reaffirmed the belief that our shared experiences can be a wellspring of inspiration, hope, and testament to the indomitable spirit of humanity. My story, while unique in its details, is a fragment of a grand tapestry of human experience. My deepest aspiration is for it to serve as a beacon, guiding others toward healing, understanding, and self-liberation. As you traverse your life's journey, remain open to the myriad guiding lights that may come your way. These beacons might manifest as words of comfort, profound realizations, or lessons from adversity. They serve as our navigational stars, offering clarity when our paths blur. By embracing the shared narratives of others, we contribute to a communal roadmap that paves the way to collective liberation. So, cherish each step, embrace the lessons, and celebrate your triumphs. You are never alone in this journey. Each story, including yours, possesses the innate power to uplift and inspire. May we all harness our narratives' strength, guiding not only ourselves but also those seeking a glimmer of hope.

Read out loud:

I am deserving. I am capable. I am strong. I am safe. I am worthy. I am enough. I am love.

I AM.

In Sinatra's notes of "My Way" I'm immersed,

As landscapes shift in rhythmic verse.

Bridges rise, then fade from sight,

Carrying memories, both dark and light.

Heart swelling with a boundless tide,

A smile so wide, I cannot hide.

A symphony of joy, gratitude so deep,

Emotions awakened from their dormant sleep.

Tears trace paths upon my face,

Celebrating life's enduring grace.

With every note, my spirit takes flight,

Soaring, unfettered, in the purest light.

For God hath not given us the spirit of fear; but of power, and love, and a sound mind.

2 TIMOTHY 1:7

"Anyone can be manipulated by a narcissist. It has nothing to do with your level of intelligence, or how many degrees you have. Victims of narcissistic abuse often feel stupid for allowing themselves to be taken advantage of by narcissists. We are not taught to protect ourselves from these predators. We are also not taught the nature of who we are dealing with. Most of us didn't know people like this existed. We were completely unprepared to deal with this insidious manipulatory abuse."

—MARIA CONSIGLIO

It's not always low self-esteem that keeps people in abusive relationships. Some people go into these relationships with high esteem and because of the chronic abuse, end up feeling terrible about themselves. Children are not born feeling like they are not good enough. Consistent abuse will not only change who a person is but it also can diminish who a person can become. When people get educated about abuse dynamics and have a better understanding of narcissism then in many instances it's the beginning of the end of these relationships. You cannot unsee the truth of who they are and you are no longer a pawn in their game. What keeps a lot of people in these relationships is a lack of knowledge about emotional and mental abuse and how it affects people. It is the deception that keeps them hostage, not necessarily just a lack of self- worth.

—Maria Consiglio

Gratitude

A myriad of cherished family, friends, and strangers have left an indelible mark on my journey, offering invaluable guidance, support, and companionship. While words may fall short of expressing the profound gratitude I feel, please know that each one of you holds a special place in my heart and narrative. I had hoped to inscribe your names, to eternally etch your unwavering integrity, kindness, and wisdom into this story. However, respecting your privacy is paramount. Each of you knows who you are, and this note stands as a humble testament to my immense appreciation. Your influence permeates every page, and more importantly, has shaped who I am today. The journey of penning this memoir brought forth a tidal wave of gratitude for the constant presence, encouragement, and faith each of you has bestowed upon me. While words are inherently limited, please regard this acknowledgment as an ode to the lasting impact you've had on my life and work. Your contributions are etched in my memory and heart. Thank you for walking alongside me on this journey. I cherish and love each of you, beyond the constraints of time and space.

PART 2

Resources

In the pages that follow, I aim to provide a comprehensive compilation of resources that I believe will significantly aid you on your journey to healing. Please understand these resources serve as a guiding compass, granting you the autonomy to choose what is personally applicable and to disregard what doesn't resonate with you. It's important to remember that each person's healing journey is unique, and a strategy that works for one might not be equally effective for another. I encourage you to approach these resources with openness and receptivity, exploring and employing them in a way that feels most genuine and helpful to you. This approach will empower you to navigate your path to recovery from trauma and abuse effectively. Your journey is deeply personal, and I hope these resources can offer some support and direction as you undertake this critical, courageous endeavor.

List of Red Flags

I Saw and Ignored | Beth Watson@ yourinnersherlock (Instagram)

Inability to admit fault
Constant excuse making
Superficial charm & flattery
Compulsive lying
Narcissistic rage
Severe guilt tripping
Financially irresponsible
Unreliable, untrustworthy, unfaithful & inconsistent
Fantasy storytelling
Empty promises
Confusing communication
Deflecting, diverting and blame-shifting conversations
Used 'intentional forgetting
Publicly pleasant & passive, privately neglectful & abusive
Words not matching actions
Grandiosity and arrogance
Heavy complaining that had no end
Secretive with phones and social media to hide supply
Inflated sense of entitlement
Threatening to leave to install fear
Exploiting the qualities of others
Using money to control & enmesh

Using seduction to control
Triangulating people to control the flow of communication
Sexually exploitative and predatory
Feeding people false stories to hide their behavior
Expected special treatment but reciprocates nothing
Speeds up relationships to enmesh
Exaggerating achievements to feel important and special
Hypocrisy and contradiction
Unphased by people's emotions
Inability to change or take accountability for his behavior
Causing arguments and drama to feel in control and superior
Lack of integrity
Emotional availability of an infant
Breadcrumbing in front of others
Mirroring and copying others
Severe victim playing
Obsessed with the opinions of others
Extreme selfishness

My Therapy Healing Plan

Through sharing my individualized therapy healing plan, I aim to convey my inherent inclination towards seeking enlightenment and embracing a holistic approach to healing. It is important to acknowledge that this plan is specific to my experiences, and there is no one-size-fits-all solution that can be universally applied. What has proven beneficial for me may not necessarily yield the same results for others. It is vital to honor and respect your unique needs, allowing yourself the space to discover what resonates with your healing journey. I deeply value the importance of individuality and encourage others to explore and embrace the strategies and practices that align best with their path to healing. The following insights provide an outline of the approaches and techniques that have supported me in my quest for healing.

Therapy

Cognitive Behavioral Therapy (CBT) is a structured and goal-oriented type of talk therapy that is widely used in psychology and counseling. It focuses on identifying and changing negative thought patterns, emotions, and behaviors to improve mental health and well-being. CBT is typically short-term and highly practical, involving collaboration between the therapist and the individual to develop coping skills, challenge and modify unhelpful beliefs, and implement positive changes in behavior. It is a widely researched and evidence-based approach that is effective in treating a variety of mental health conditions, including anxiety, depression, and stress-related disorders.

EMDR (Eye Movement Desensitization and Reprocessing) Therapy is a form of psychotherapy developed by Francine Shapiro in the 1980s. It was initially designed to address the distress associated with traumatic memories, such as those experienced in post-traumatic stress disorder (PTSD). EMDR is a unique therapeutic approach that involves the use of bilateral stimulation, such as eye movements, hand taps, or auditory tones, to facilitate the reprocessing of traumatic memories and the integration of adaptive beliefs and emotions. The goal of EMDR is to help individuals process traumatic experiences in a safe and controlled manner, reducing the emotional distress associated with those memories and promoting healing and resolution. EMDR has been widely used and researched for its effectiveness in treating various mental health conditions, including PTSD, anxiety, phobias, and other trauma-related disorders. It is a recognized and evidence-based therapy that has helped many individuals overcome the effects of traumatic experiences and improve their mental well-being.

Massage

Lymphatic Massage, also known as lymphatic drainage massage, is a specialized form of massage therapy that focuses on stimulating the lymphatic system. The lymphatic system plays a crucial role in maintaining the body's immune function, eliminating toxins, and transporting fluids throughout the body. Lymphatic massage aims to promote the flow of lymph fluid, reduce swelling, and enhance the body's natural detoxification process. During a lymphatic massage session, a trained therapist uses gentle, rhythmic strokes and light pressure to stimulate the lymph nodes and encourage lymphatic fluid circulation. The massage techniques used are usually slow, repetitive, and directed towards specific areas of the body where lymphatic congestion may occur, such as the neck, armpits, and groin. The therapist may also incorporate breathing techniques and stretching movements to enhance the effectiveness of the massage.

Lymphatic massage can offer various benefits, including:

- Reducing swelling and edema: Lymphatic massage can help alleviate swelling and fluid retention caused by conditions like lymphedema, post-surgery recovery, or injury.
- Boosting immune function: By enhancing lymphatic flow, the massage can support the immune system and improve the body's ability to fight infections and illnesses.
- Detoxification: Lymphatic massage can aid in the removal of toxins, waste products, and metabolic byproducts from the body, promoting overall detoxification.
- Relaxation and stress relief: The gentle and soothing nature of lymphatic massage can induce deep relaxation, reduce stress, and promote a sense of calm and well-being.
- Improving circulation: By stimulating lymphatic flow, the massage can also enhance blood circulation, delivering oxygen and nutrients to tissues while removing metabolic waste.

It's important to note that lymphatic massage may not be suitable for everyone, such as individuals with certain medical conditions or infections. It's advisable to consult with a qualified healthcare professional or a licensed massage therapist to determine if lymphatic massage is appropriate for your specific needs. Overall, lymphatic massage can be a beneficial therapy for those seeking to support their lymphatic system, reduce swelling, enhance detoxification, and promote overall well-being.

Reiki

Reiki is a form of alternative healing therapy that originated in Japan. The word "Reiki" is derived from two Japanese words: "rei" meaning universal or spiritual, and "ki" meaning life force energy. Reiki practitioners believe that there is a life force energy that flows through all living beings, and when this energy is low or blocked, it can lead to physical, emotional, and spiritual imbalances or ailments. Reiki is based on the concept of channeling this life force energy to promote healing, relaxation, and overall well-being. The practitioner acts as a conduit for the energy and uses their hands to direct and transmit the energy to the recipient. During a Reiki session, the recipient remains fully clothed and typically lies down on a massage table, while the practitioner places their hands lightly on or near the body in different positions.

The benefits of Reiki can vary from person to person, but some commonly reported effects include:

- Relaxation and stress reduction: Reiki promotes deep relaxation, which can help alleviate stress, anxiety, and tension.
- Pain management: Reiki may help reduce pain and discomfort, promoting a sense of ease and comfort.
- Emotional healing: Reiki can support emotional healing by releasing blocked or suppressed emotions, promoting emotional balance, and providing a sense of inner peace.
- Enhanced well-being: Reiki is believed to balance and harmonize the energy centers in the body (known as chakras), promoting overall physical, mental, and emotional well-being.
- Improved energy flow: Reiki aims to remove energy blockages and restore the healthy flow of life force energy throughout the body, supporting vitality and promoting a sense of vitality.

Meditation

Meditation is a practice that has no right or wrong way. For me, I have created a personal space by my window with a bolster, and I commit to sitting and focusing on my breath. On some days, I may engage in mantra or affirmation meditation, while other times I may follow a guided meditation that resonates with me, which I can find on various streaming services. I don't enforce any specific time commitment on myself, as I believe meditation is a personal practice that can be flexible and adaptable to my needs and preferences. The key is to create a space that feels comfortable and conducive to meditation and to find a practice that works for me in the moment. Meditation is a powerful tool for relaxation, mindfulness, and self-awareness, and it can be tailored to suit individual preferences and needs.

Breathwork

The Two-Part Breath, also known as Holotropic Breathwork, is a powerful technique that offers numerous benefits. These may include reducing stress or tension, increasing energy levels, stabilizing heart rate, regulating the nervous system, improving sleep, enhancing mood and overall well-being, and reducing anxiety, sadness, or anger. The class I took was specifically designed to settle the nervous system through focused breathing techniques. The intention was to create an optimal environment for releasing stress, tension, trauma, and stored emotions from the brain and body. This release allowed for a newfound space to meet ourselves in a new light, unencumbered by past emotional baggage. Through the power of breath, we were able to return to ourselves fully. The practice of Two-Part Breath or Holotropic Breathwork can be a profound and transformative experience, helping us tap into our inner resources and heal on multiple levels, including the physical, emotional, and spiritual realms.

Sound bath meditation

Sound bath meditation is a unique and immersive experience that has numerous benefits for the mind and body. During a sound bath, the brainwave state is altered from the normal waking state (beta) to a more relaxed state (alpha), dreamlike state (theta), and even a restorative state (delta). This altered state of consciousness allows for deep relaxation and can lead to various positive effects. As the mind and body relax during a sound bath, the heart rate and blood pressure tend to decrease, and breathing becomes deeper. This can help to promote a sense of calm and relaxation throughout the entire body. The focus on the present moment and the clearing of distractions during a sound bath can help to quiet the mind and promote mental clarity.

One of the notable benefits of sound bath meditation is its potential to help release negative emotions such as anger and frustration. The soothing sounds and vibrations from various instruments used in a sound bath, such as singing bowls, gongs, or drums, can help to release tension and promote emotional healing. Moreover, the deep states of relaxation achieved during a sound bath can also have a positive impact on sleep quality. By reducing stress levels and promoting relaxation, sound bath meditation can help improve sleep patterns, leading to better overall sleep quality. In addition to these benefits, sound bath meditation has been reported to improve moods, reduce anxiety and stress, and promote a sense of well-being. It is a holistic practice that engages the senses, creating a unique and transformative experience for the mind, body, and spirit.

Yoga

Yoga has been recognized as a powerful tool for healing from trauma, as it addresses the interconnectedness of the mind, body, and spirit. The practice of yoga, including physical postures (asanas), breathwork (pranayama), mindfulness, and meditation, can have a profound impact on individuals who have experienced trauma. One of the primary ways in which yoga can support healing from trauma is by helping to regulate the nervous system. Trauma can often leave the nervous system in a state of dysregulation, with heightened levels of stress, anxiety, and tension. The practice of yoga, with its emphasis on deep breathing, gentle movements, and mindfulness, can activate the relaxation response of the nervous system, promoting a sense of calm and safety. Yoga can also help individuals connect with their bodies in a positive and empowering way. Trauma can often result in a disconnection from the body, as individuals may have experienced sensations of pain, discomfort, or numbness during the traumatic event. Through yoga, individuals can learn to inhabit their bodies with mindfulness and cultivate a sense of embodiment, helping to rebuild a positive relationship with their physical selves. Overall, the practice of yoga can have a profound impact on healing from trauma by regulating the nervous system, promoting embodiment, supporting emotional processing and release, and fostering self-care and self-compassion. It is important to note that trauma healing is a complex and individual process, and yoga should be approached with sensitivity, awareness, and the guidance of a qualified and experienced teacher or therapist.

Journaling

Journaling can be a powerful tool for healing from trauma, as it provides a safe and private space for individuals to express and process their thoughts, emotions, and experiences.

Emotional expression: Trauma often leaves individuals with intense emotions that can be difficult to process. Journaling provides a space for individuals to freely express their emotions without judgment or inhibition. It allows them to put their thoughts and feelings into words, which can help in acknowledging, understanding, and processing their emotions.

Reflection and self-awareness: Journaling encourages self-reflection and self-awareness, which are essential for healing from trauma. It allows individuals to gain insight into their thoughts, behaviors, and patterns of reactions. Through journaling, individuals can explore their triggers, reactions, and coping mechanisms, gaining a deeper understanding of themselves and their trauma-related responses.

Creating a narrative: Journaling can help individuals create a narrative around their trauma. It allows them to organize their thoughts and experiences, create meaning, and make sense of their trauma story. This can provide a sense of coherence and understanding, which can be empowering and healing.

Processing and integrating memories: Trauma memories can be fragmented, disjointed, and overwhelming. Journaling can assist individuals in processing and integrating these memories in a safe and structured manner. Writing about the traumatic event(s), their impact, and the emotions associated with them can help individuals process and integrate their memories into their life stories.

Coping and self-care: Journaling can serve as a coping mechanism and a form of self-care for individuals healing from trauma. It provides an outlet for stress, anxiety, and overwhelming emotions. It can also serve as a tool for self-soothing, self-nurturing, and self-compassion, as individuals can write kind and supportive messages to themselves.

Monitoring progress: Journaling allows individuals to track their progress over time. It can be a tangible record of their healing journey, showing them how far they have come and providing motivation to continue their healing work. It's important to note that journaling may not be suitable for everyone, and it is important to approach it with self-compassion and self-care. If journaling triggers distress or becomes overwhelming, it is recommended to seek support from a qualified therapist or counselor. Journaling should be used as a tool in conjunction with other appropriate therapeutic interventions for healing from trauma.

Making Amends

As I engaged in the process of introspection and reflection, I began to recognize the profound impact that my experiences had on the relationships in my life. The weight of the connections that had been strained or broken weighed heavily on my heart. In an earnest effort to address these ruptured bonds, I took it upon myself to write letters of apology, expressing my genuine desire for reconciliation. However, I approached this endeavor without any expectations, fully acknowledging and respecting the autonomy of the individuals involved. The crucial aspect for me was to assume personal accountability and convey heartfelt remorse for any pain or hurt my actions may have caused. While it was never my intention to purposefully sever these connections or inflict harm upon my friends, once I became aware of the potential impact, I felt a strong compulsion to make amends.

Music

Using music for healing from trauma can be a powerful tool, and incorporating positive affirmations and specific frequencies can enhance its effectiveness. Here are some ways in which using music with positive affirmations and Hz frequencies can be beneficial for trauma healing:

Grounding and centering: Music can help individuals feel grounded and centered, providing a sense of stability and security, especially during times of heightened anxiety or distress. Positive affirmations can further reinforce positive thoughts and beliefs, helping individuals shift their mindset towards more empowering perspectives.

Emotional regulation: Music can evoke emotions, and by choosing music with positive affirmations and specific Hz frequencies, individuals can intentionally regulate their emotions. For example, Hz music, such as 432 Hz or 528 Hz, is believed to have healing properties and can help individuals relax, reduce stress, and promote a sense of well-being.

Intention setting: Choosing specific frequencies based on intention can be a powerful way to set positive intentions for healing from trauma. For example, 528 Hz is associated with DNA repair and is believed to promote healing and transformation, while 432 Hz is said to have a calming effect on the mind and body. By intentionally selecting music with specific frequencies, individuals can set the tone for their healing journey and enhance their overall well-being.

Background support: Playing music with positive affirmations and Hz frequencies in the background while working or engaging in other activities can provide ongoing support for trauma healing. It can create a soothing and supportive environment, promoting a sense of calmness and relaxation throughout the day.

Personalization: Choosing artists or musicians that resonate with an individual's personal preferences can create a meaningful and personalized experience. Coax Marie, or any other artist who brings comfort and inspiration, can serve as a source of comfort and inspiration during the healing process.

Frequency List

Have fun exploring Hz music and all the findings—I hope it resonates with you!

- 174 Hz: Known as the healing frequency, it is believed to help reduce pain, tension, and stress, and promote overall healing and well-being.
- 285 Hz: Traditionally associated with healing of the root chakra, it is believed to help balance and stabilize the root chakra, which is associated with a sense of safety, security, and grounding.
- 396 Hz: Thought to aid in reducing or eliminating fear-based thinking, this frequency is believed to promote a sense of peace, liberation from fear, and inner healing.
- 417 Hz: Associated with releasing negativity and healing trauma, this frequency is believed to help release emotional blockages, promote emotional healing, and facilitate positive changes.
- 432 Hz: Referred to as "the heartbeat of the Earth," this frequency is believed to be in harmony with the natural vibrations of the universe, and is associated with promoting relaxation, balance, and overall well-being.
- 528 Hz: Sometimes called "the love frequency" or "the miracle tone," it is believed to promote healing, restoration, and transformation. It is also associated with the solar plexus chakra, which is related to personal power, self-confidence, and self-worth.

It's important to note that while these frequencies are often used in sound healing practices and are believed to have positive effects on the mind, body, and spirit, scientific evidence supporting their healing properties is limited.

Walking

Just getting outside in the fresh air and sun is magic. This also allows time and space for your mind to decompress. Walking can be a beneficial activity for trauma healing, as it has several potential benefits for the mind, body, and spirit.

Physical activity: Walking is a form of physical exercise that can help release tension, reduce stress, and promote overall physical well-being. Regular physical activity, including walking, has been shown to boost mood, improve sleep, and reduce symptoms of anxiety and depression, which can be beneficial for those healing from trauma.

Mindfulness: Walking can be a mindful activity that allows you to connect with your surroundings, focus on your senses, and be present in the moment. Engaging in mindful walking can help you practice grounding techniques, reduce racing thoughts, and increase your awareness of the present moment, which can help manage symptoms of trauma.

Nature connection: Walking in nature or other serene environments can have a calming effect on the mind and body. Nature has been shown to have therapeutic effects, including reducing stress and promoting well-being. Walking in nature can provide a sense of peace, tranquility, and connection with the natural world, which can support healing from trauma.

Emotional release: Walking can be a form of physical movement that allows you to release built up emotions. It can provide a safe outlet for processing emotions related to trauma, such as anger, sadness, or anxiety. Walking can also stimulate the production of endorphins, which are natural mood-enhancing chemicals in the brain that can help boost your mood and promote emotional healing.

Self-care: Taking time for self-care is an important aspect of trauma healing. Walking can be a form of self-care that allows you to prioritize your physical and mental well-being. It can be an act of self-nurturing, self-compassion, and self-empowerment, as you take steps towards healing and self-recovery.

Weightlifting at the Gym

Engaging in physical exercises, such as going to the gym, can be a beneficial component of a holistic approach to healing from trauma. Trauma can have significant impacts on both the mind and body. Incorporating physical exercise into one's healing journey can have several potential benefits:

Release of endorphins: Exercise can trigger the release of endorphins, which are chemicals in the brain that can help improve mood, reduce stress, and increase feelings of well-being. This can be particularly helpful for individuals who may be struggling with symptoms of depression, anxiety, or other emotional distress related to trauma.

Regulation of the nervous system: Trauma can disrupt the body's natural regulation of the nervous system, leading to symptoms such as hypervigilance, flashbacks, and difficulty sleeping. Engaging in regular exercise can help regulate the nervous system, promoting a sense of calm and relaxation.

Empowerment and self-care: Engaging in physical exercise, such as going to the gym, can be an empowering act of self-care. It allows individuals to take control of their physical health and well-being, which can positively impact their mental and emotional well-being as well.

Increased body awareness: Trauma can sometimes lead to dissociation or disconnection from the body. Engaging in physical exercise can help individuals develop a greater sense of body awareness, reconnect with their bodies, and foster a sense of embodiment.

Social support: Going to the gym can provide an opportunity for social interaction and support, which can be important for individuals healing from trauma. Connecting with others who share similar interests and goals can help reduce feelings of isolation and build a supportive community.

Time with My Tribe

Spending present and intentional time with those you love can increase your joy and gratitude. Spending time with your tribe, which refers to the people you love and care about, can be a powerful way to support your healing from trauma.

Social support: Spending time with loved ones can provide social support, which is crucial for healing from trauma. Social support can help reduce feelings of isolation, provide a sense of belonging, and offer emotional comfort. It can also provide opportunities for sharing and processing emotions related to the trauma, and receiving validation and understanding from others.

Connection and bonding: Spending intentional time with your tribe can foster connection and bonding, which can increase joy and gratitude. Engaging in activities together, sharing laughter, creating memories, and expressing affection can strengthen the bonds with your loved ones and create positive experiences that counteract the negative effects of trauma.

Distraction and enjoyment: Spending time with your tribe can be a healthy distraction from the challenges and triggers associated with trauma. Engaging in enjoyable activities with your loved ones can provide a reprieve from distressing thoughts or emotions, and create moments of joy, fun, and laughter. This can contribute to an overall sense of well-being and gratitude.

Love and validation: Being surrounded by those who love and care about you can provide validation and affirmation of your worth and value as a person. This can counteract any negative self-beliefs or doubts that may arise as a result of trauma. Feeling loved, accepted, and appreciated by your tribe can increase joy and gratitude in your life.

Shared values and meaning: Spending time with your tribe can also provide opportunities for shared values and meaning. Engaging in activities that hold personal significance, such as cultural or spiritual practices, volunteering, or participating in meaningful traditions, can foster a sense of purpose and gratitude. It can also provide a sense of belonging and connection to something greater than yourself.

Resources + Education on Abuse

Not all abuse is physical. Abuse can take many forms beyond physical, including emotional, psychological, verbal, sexual, financial, and more. It can occur concurrently in multiple forms and has severe and lasting effects.

Physical abuse involves intentional bodily harm, such as slapping, pinching, choking, kicking, shoving, or inappropriate use of drugs or physical restraints.

Emotional abuse can take various forms, including verbal abuse (such as yelling, insults, and swearing), rejection (constant dismissal of thoughts and ideas), gaslighting (manipulating truth to make one doubt their feelings and thoughts), and giving the silent treatment (intentional removal of love as a form of punishment). These abusive behaviors are used to maintain power and control over someone and can have damaging effects on mental and emotional well-being.

Mental abuse involves the use of threats, verbal insults, and other subtle tactics to control a person's thoughts and perception of reality. This form of abuse is particularly damaging as it targets self-esteem, confidence, and personal sense of competence. It can have long-term effects on mental and emotional well-being, leading to a sense of confusion, self-doubt, and loss of identity.

Financial abuse is a tactic used by abusers to exert power and control in a relationship, and it can take various forms, ranging from subtle to overt. Some examples of financial abuse include:

1. Concealing information about financial assets or accounts from the victim.
2. Limiting the victim's access to money or financial resources.
3. Stealing money or belongings from the victim.
4. Taking away pension payments or other benefits that rightfully belong to the victim.
5. Demanding payment in exchange for spending time together or visiting.
6. Sabotaging the victim's employment or financial opportunities.

Financial abuse can have serious consequences for the victim, including financial dependence, economic instability, and difficulties in leaving an abusive relationship.

Verbal abuse encompasses a wide range of words and behaviors that are used to manipulate, intimidate, and exert power and control over another person. Some examples of verbal abuse include:

1. Insults, name-calling, and derogatory remarks.
2. Humiliation, ridicule, and belittling.
3. The silent treatment, involves ignoring or refusing to communicate with the victim as a form of punishment.
4. Attempts to scare, intimidate, or threaten the victim.
5. Isolating the victim from support systems, such as friends or family.
6. Controlling behaviors, such as monitoring or dictating the victim's actions or decisions.

Verbal abuse can have serious psychological and emotional effects on the victim, including low self-esteem, anxiety, depression, and trauma.

Sexual abuse is a form of abuse that involves sexual behavior or acts forced upon a person without their consent. It can occur to individuals of any gender, age, or relationship. Sexual abuse can include various forms of sexual misconduct, assault, or exploitation, and it can be perpetrated by individuals of any gender or age.

Sexual abuse can take many forms, including but not limited to:

1. **Rape or sexual assault**: non-consensual sexual activity, including penetration or other sexual acts, without the victim's consent.
2. **Inappropriate touching or groping**: unwanted touching of intimate areas of the body without consent.
3. **Sexual harassment**: unwanted sexual advances, comments, or behavior that creates a hostile or uncomfortable environment.
4. **Child sexual abuse**: sexual activity or exploitation involving a child, including molestation, grooming, or child pornography.
5. **Sexual coercion**: pressuring or manipulating a person into engaging in sexual activity against their will.

Sexual abuse is a grave infringement upon a person's rights and can result in profound and enduring psychological, emotional, and physical repercussions.

Psychological abuse involves the repeated and intentional use of words, actions, and behaviors to manipulate, hurt, weaken, or frighten someone mentally and emotionally. It can also involve distorting, confusing, or influencing a person's thoughts and actions within their daily life, resulting in changes to their sense of self and overall well-being. Psychological abuse can take many forms, including but not limited to:

1. **Verbal abuse**: using harsh, insulting, or derogatory language to belittle or demean a person.
2. **Emotional manipulation**: manipulating a person's emotions or feelings to gain power and control over them.
3. **Gaslighting**: manipulating a person's perception of reality, making them doubt their thoughts, feelings, or experiences.
4. **Threats and intimidation**: using threats or intimidation to instill fear and control in a person.
5. **Isolation**: restricting or limiting a person's access to social support systems or isolating them from friends, family, or other sources of support.
6. **Controlling behaviors**: exerting control over a person's thoughts, actions, or decisions through monitoring, surveillance, or manipulation.
7. **Humiliation and ridicule**: intentionally humiliating or mocking a person to undermine their self-esteem and confidence.

Psychological abuse can have severe and long-lasting effects on a person's mental, emotional, and physical well-being.

All the forms of abuse mentioned, including physical, emotional, mental, financial, sexual, and psychological abuse, are equally damaging and harmful. Abuse can take many different forms and can be perpetrated in various combinations by an abuser to gain power and control over their victim. It is important to understand that abuse is never acceptable in any form and all forms of abuse are equally serious and damaging to the well-being and safety of the victim. If you or someone you know is experiencing any form of abuse, it is crucial to seek help and support from trusted individuals or professional resources. The effects of physical abuse can have long-lasting and detrimental impacts on an individual's physical and mental health. Chronic health problems such as heart problems, high blood pressure, and digestive problems can result from the physical injuries inflicted during abuse. Additionally, the psychological and emotional toll of physical abuse can lead to the development of mental health issues such as depression, anxiety, and eating disorders. Coping mechanisms, such as alcohol or drug misuse, may also be employed by survivors of physical abuse as a way to cope with the trauma they have experienced. It is essential to recognize that the effects of physical abuse can extend beyond the immediate injuries and can have long-term consequences on an individual's overall well-being. Seeking support from trusted professionals and resources is crucial for survivors of physical abuse to address and heal from the physical and emotional impacts of abuse.

Hotlines:

National Domestic Violence Hotline: 800-799-7233
National Sexual Assault Hotline: 1-800-656-4673
Suicide and Crisis Lifeline: 988

Resources + Education on Narcissistic Abuse

Narcissistic abuse refers to a type of psychological abuse inflicted by individuals with narcissistic personality traits or narcissistic personality disorder (NPD). It involves a pattern of manipulative and harmful behaviors aimed at controlling, demeaning, and exploiting others for the narcissist's gain. Narcissistic abuse can occur in various forms, including emotional, verbal, psychological, and sometimes even physical abuse. It often results in profound and long-lasting negative effects on the victim's mental, emotional, and physical well-being, including low self-esteem, anxiety, depression, post-traumatic stress disorder (PTSD), and other psychological and emotional challenges. It is important to seek support and professional help if you believe you may be a victim of narcissistic abuse.

Narcissist: a person who exhibits traits such as a lack of empathy, manipulative behavior, gaslighting (making others doubt their reality), incessant lying, and believing their lies. They often make others doubt their emotions and may label them as "crazy" or "insane". They may also engage in rage or anger outbursts without apparent reason, leading the victim to apologize or feel responsible. Narcissists can be found in various relationships, including parents, friends, siblings, bosses, or spouses. In the beginning, they may "love bomb" their victims with excessive affection and charm, but over time, they may begin to abuse and manipulate the victim to gain control. This can include isolating the victim from their family and friends, further exacerbating the victim's sense of helplessness and dependence on the narcissist. It's important to recognize the signs of narcissistic abuse and seek support from trusted sources to break free from the cycle of abuse and regain control over one's own life.

Covert Narcissists often appear as sensitive and caring individuals, which can make people feel comfortable being vulnerable with them. However, this is a manipulative tactic to gain your trust. They may use the personal information they learn about you to slowly and insidiously erode your self-esteem, either through passive-aggressive behavior or other sneaky tactics. Some victims may not even realize what is happening due to the covert and insidious nature of the abuse, which is why it is often called hidden abuse.

The Signs

True narcissistic abuse has a very distinct and consistent pattern:

Lack of Ownership or Responsibility: The abuser consistently avoids taking ownership or responsibility for their actions, words, or behavior. They often shift blame onto you, claiming that you misunderstood or that you are too sensitive or incapable of taking a joke.

Arguments over Sharing Feelings or Needs: Whenever you try to express your feelings, desires, or needs, it quickly turns into an argument. Even simple matters become sources of conflict, leaving you feeling unheard and invalidated.

Gaslighting: You constantly feel like your reality is being questioned. The abuser undermines your perceptions, making you doubt yourself and believe that everything is your fault. They may dismiss your feelings as oversensitivity or an overreaction.

Anxiety and Mental Distress: You experience symptoms such as anxiety, rapid heartbeat, racing thoughts, and replaying confusing interactions in an attempt to make sense of what went wrong in conversations with the abuser.

Feeling like You're Losing Your Sanity: In the context of the relationship with this particular individual, you feel as though you're losing your mind. Yet, in other relationships or situations, you don't experience the same emotional turmoil. Others perceive you as stable, articulate, and intelligent, further intensifying the confusion and isolation of the abusive relationship

It's important to note that narcissistic abuse can have various forms and severity levels, and seeking support from a trusted friend, family member, or professional may be helpful if you're experiencing any of these signs in a relationship.

Narcissists use controlling behavior as a way to maintain power and dominance over their victims. One of the tactics they use is interrupting you when you speak or speaking over you. This tactic is intended to undermine your voice and make you feel like what you have to say is unimportant. When a narcissist interrupts you or speaks over you, it sends the message that they don't value your opinion and that their needs and desires are more important than yours.

Another way narcissists use controlling behavior is by not allowing you to finish your sentences. They may do this by cutting you off mid-sentence or by redirecting the conversation to something else before you have a chance to express your thoughts fully. This tactic is designed to keep you off balance and prevent you from having a say in the conversation.

Narcissists may also use dominant body language or raise their voice to intimidate you and make you feel small and powerless. This can include standing over you, invading your personal space, or using aggressive gestures such as pointing or finger-wagging. When a narcissist uses dominant body language or raises their voice, it sends the message that they are in control and that you are powerless to resist their demands.

Narcissists often use a variety of tactics to minimize the voices of others, including gaslighting, projecting, and blame-shifting. Gaslighting is a tactic in which the narcissist makes the victim question their reality and perception of events. The narcissist might deny that certain events took place, or distort the truth to cast themselves in a favorable light and make the victim appear at fault. This can make the victim feel like they are going crazy or that their feelings and thoughts are invalid.

Projection is another tactic narcissists use to minimize the voices of others. This involves the narcissist projecting their negative traits and behaviors onto the victim. For example, when the victim raises concerns about the narcissist's behavior, the narcissist might counter-accuse the victim of being controlling or manipulative. This can lead the victim to feel guilty or ashamed, causing them to doubt their own thoughts and feelings.

Blame-shifting is a tactic narcissists use to shift responsibility for their actions onto the victim. For instance, if caught lying or cheating, the narcissist might blame the victim for lacking trust or failing to meet their needs. This tactic can lead the victim to feel as though they are to blame for the narcissist's behavior, potentially causing them to suppress their own feelings to avoid conflict or additional blame.

Triangulation is a manipulative tactic commonly employed by narcissists to sow discord and maintain control in relationships. It involves the narcissist bringing a third person into a situation, often pitting them against the victim, to create conflict, insecurity, jealousy, and a sense of competition. The third party can be anyone, such as a family member, friend, or even a new romantic interest. By involving a third party, the narcissist seeks to undermine the victim's confidence, create doubt in their perceptions, and exert power and dominance over them. This psychological manipulation can have devastating effects on the victim's self-esteem, trust, and overall well-being.

All of these tactics are designed to minimize your voice and make you feel like you don't have a say in the relationship. Narcissists want to be in control at all times, and they will use whatever means necessary to maintain their power and dominance. It's important to recognize these behaviors for what they are and to take steps to protect yourself from their manipulations.

Here is a list of gaslighting statements that may be used by narcissists:

1. "I was just joking."
2. "I didn't do that."
3. "You're imagining things."

4. "You were there with us."
5. "You make things up in your head."
6. "I never said that."
7. "Well, if that's what you got from what I said."
8. "Don't be so sensitive."
9. "You have issues."
10. "You're upset over nothing."
11. "You always do this."
12. "Stop imagining things."
13. "You need help."
14. "It's always something with you."
15. "Here we go again."
16. "No one likes you."
17. "They're lying."
18. "I don't have time for this."
19. "There is always drama with you."

It's important to recognize that gaslighting is a form of psychological manipulation used by narcissists to undermine and invalidate the experiences and perceptions of others. It is meant to distort reality, create confusion, and exert control over the victim. If you are experiencing gaslighting in a relationship, it's crucial to seek support from trusted friends, family, or mental health professionals, and to set healthy boundaries to protect your well-being. Gaslighting is not acceptable behavior, and it's important to prioritize your mental health and safety in any relationship.

Here are some ways a narcissist may react when called out:

1. **Gaslighting**: They may claim that you misunderstood them or deny any knowledge of the situation, making you question your perceptions and reality.
2. **Deflection**: They may talk over you, accuse you of interrupting, or claim that you never let them finish, shifting the blame away from themselves.
3. **Manipulation**: They may try to provoke a reaction from you by pushing your buttons or using tactics to elicit an emotional response, diverting attention from their behavior.
4. **Blame- shifting and shaming**: hey might shift blame to you or use shaming tactics, leading you to feel guilty or as if you're responsible for their actions.
5. **Rage and Accusations**: They may respond with anger or rage, blaming you for "making them" behave that way and accusing you of enjoying it.
6. **Property Damage:** They may damage property and then deny intent to hurt you, minimizing their behavior or claiming it was accidental.
7. **Victim Blaming**: They may accuse you of causing their abusive behavior, claiming that you made them do it or provoked them.
8. **Physical Violence**: In extreme cases, they may become physically violent, such as strangling you, and then blame you for their actions.

It's important to recognize that these reactions are manipulative tactics used by narcissists to deflect responsibility and maintain control. If you are experiencing any form of abuse, it's crucial to prioritize your safety and seek support from trusted individuals or professionals.

Manipulation + Narcissistic Abuse

Countering is a form of **psychological manipulation** that is often used by narcissists to control and dominate their victims. It is a dangerous abuse tactic that can leave victims feeling confused, invalidated, and powerless. Here are five signs that you may be experiencing countering:

1. **Your experiences and emotions are minimized or denied.**

   Narcissists might dismiss your feelings as invalid or accuse you of overreacting. They can also deny or downplay events, causing you to question your own experiences and emotions, and making you feel as if you're losing your grip on reality.

2. **Your words are twisted or misconstrued.**

   Narcissists may take your words out of context or twist their meaning to suit their agenda. They may also use your words against you, repeating them back to you in a way that makes you look bad or invalidates your point of view. This can leave you feeling as though you are unable to communicate effectively or that your words have no value.

3. **You are accused of things you didn't do.**

   Narcissists may accuse you of things that you did not do or that are completely untrue. This is a way for them to deflect attention away from their behavior and to make you feel guilty or ashamed. They may also use this tactic to control you or to make you feel as though you are always in the wrong.

4. **You are constantly corrected or contradicted.**

   Narcissists may constantly correct or contradict you, even on the most minor things. This is a way for them to assert their dominance and to make you feel as though you are always wrong. They may also do this to make themselves look better or to maintain control over the conversation.

5. **You feel as though you are walking on eggshells.**

   Countering can make you feel as though you are constantly walking on eggshells, never knowing when you will be corrected or contradicted. This can lead to anxiety, depression, and a loss of self-esteem. You may also begin to second-guess yourself and to doubt your judgment.

If you recognize any of these signs in your life, it's essential to seek help and support. A therapist or counselor can assist you in developing strategies to cope, counteract the abuse, and reclaim your power and voice.

Signs you are Being Manipulated

- You are afraid to disagree.
- You often feel anxious and fearful.
- You hesitate to set boundaries.
- You are plagued by constant feelings of guilt.
- You experience persistent confusion.
- You can never truly relax.
- Their actions and words don't align (e.g., they mistreat you but then claim to love you).
- You feel as though you're losing your sanity.
- The manipulator frequently twists, minimizes, or invalidates your statements.
- They punish you for not complying with their wishes.
- They insult you but always have an excuse (e.g., "It was just a joke," "You're too sensitive," "You misunderstood me").

Note on Mental Health + Narcissistic Abuse

While there is not a specific type of brain damage associated with narcissistic abuse, prolonged exposure to this type of abuse can have significant negative impacts on mental health and well-being. Narcissistic abuse can lead to conditions such as depression, anxiety, post-traumatic stress disorder (PTSD), and complex PTSD. These conditions can cause changes in brain structure and function, such as alterations in the amygdala, hippocampus, and prefrontal cortex, which are involved in emotion regulation, memory, and decision-making. Studies have shown that chronic stress, which is often a result of prolonged exposure to narcissistic abuse, can lead to damage in the brain, including the shrinking of the hippocampus and prefrontal cortex. These areas are important for memory, learning, decision-making, and emotion regulation. Stress can also cause an increase in cortisol, a hormone associated with stress, which can cause damage to the brain over time. Furthermore, narcissistic abuse can have a significant impact on a person's sense of self and identity. This can lead to feelings of confusion, self-doubt, and low self-esteem, which can further impact mental health and well-being. The experience of being constantly invalidated and gaslighted can cause a person to question their reality and perception, leading to a loss of trust in oneself and others. It is important to seek help and support if you are experiencing narcissistic abuse or have experienced it in the past. Therapy can help you work through the effects of abuse and develop healthy coping mechanisms. Additionally, self-care practices such as mindfulness, exercise, and social support can help mitigate the negative effects of chronic stress on the brain and mental health. It's important to note, however, that not everyone who experiences narcissistic abuse will develop brain-related issues. Resilience, coping strategies, and seeking support can all play a role in mitigating the negative effects of trauma. If you are concerned about the impact of narcissistic abuse on your mental health, it may be helpful to speak with a mental health professional. If you have experienced narcissistic abuse and are struggling with your mental health, here are some ways to help:

Seek therapy: Consider working with a mental health professional who has experience in treating trauma and abuse. They can provide support, validation, and tools for coping with the aftermath of narcissistic abuse.

Practice self-care: It's essential to prioritize self-care to help manage stress and anxiety. Make time for activities that bring you joy and relaxation, such as exercise, meditation, journaling, or spending time in nature.

Set boundaries: One of the most challenging aspects of recovering from narcissistic abuse is setting boundaries with the abuser and others who may have enabled or ignored the abuse. Work with your therapist or coach to identify healthy boundaries and practice enforcing them.

Connect with support groups: Finding a community of others who have experienced similar abuse can be healing and validating. Consider joining a support group, either online or in person.

Educate yourself: Learning about narcissistic abuse and its effects on mental health can help you understand and validate your experiences.

Remember, healing from narcissistic abuse takes time and patience. Be gentle with yourself and focus on taking small steps towards your recovery every day.

PTSD + Narcissistic Abuse

PTSD (Post-Traumatic Stress Disorder) from narcissistic abuse can manifest in a variety of ways. Some common symptoms of PTSD include:

Intrusive Thoughts: Intrusive thoughts are unwanted, often disturbing thoughts or memories that repeatedly enter your mind. For someone who has experienced narcissistic abuse, these intrusive thoughts might involve flashbacks to the abuse, nightmares, or other distressing memories.

Hypervigilance: Hypervigilance is a state of increased alertness and sensitivity to potential threats. After experiencing narcissistic abuse, you may find yourself constantly on edge, scanning your environment for signs of danger.

Avoidance: Avoidance is a coping mechanism that involves avoiding people, places, or situations that remind you of the traumatic event. Someone who has experienced narcissistic abuse might avoid social situations, certain places, or even certain topics of conversation to avoid triggering memories of the abuse.

Emotional Numbness: Emotional numbness is a common symptom of PTSD. It involves feeling disconnected from your emotions, or feeling as though you are unable to feel emotions at all. This may be a way to cope with the overwhelming emotions that come with the aftermath of narcissistic abuse.

Hyperarousal: Hyperarousal is a state of heightened arousal that can involve irritability, difficulty sleeping, and an exaggerated startle response. Someone who has experienced narcissistic abuse may be hypervigilant and easily startled, leading to feelings of anxiety and difficulty sleeping.

It's important to note that not everyone who experiences narcissistic abuse will develop PTSD, and not everyone with PTSD will experience the same symptoms. If you suspect that you may be experiencing PTSD as a result of narcissistic abuse, it's important to seek professional help from a therapist or mental health professional.

Resources for Continued Reading

Reading books related to self-growth, spirituality, mindfulness, relationships, and career development can be a great way to gain insights, guidance, and tools for personal transformation and empowerment. However, it's important to approach these books with an open mind and discernment, and to choose those that resonate with your journey and personal beliefs.

The Inner Work by Mat & Ash—This book provides insights and practical exercises for inner growth, healing, and self-discovery.

A Course in Miracles by Foundation for Inner Peace—This book offers a spiritual framework for personal transformation and a deeper understanding of the nature of reality.

Oneness by Rasha—This book explores the concept of oneness and offers practical guidance for living a more spiritually fulfilling life.

Conversations with God by Neale Donald Walsch—This book offers a series of dialogues between the author and God, offering insights and perspectives on life, love, and spirituality.

Set Boundaries, Find Peace by Nedra Glover Tawwab—This book provides guidance on setting and enforcing healthy boundaries in relationships.

Open Heart, Clear Mind by Thubten Chodron—This book offers practical guidance on meditation and mindfulness practices for cultivating inner peace and happiness.

Freedom & Resolve by Gangaji—This book explores the nature of freedom and offers insights into overcoming the limitations of the mind and ego.

Career Confinement by Elizabeth Pearson—This book provides guidance on finding career fulfillment and overcoming self-limiting beliefs and behaviors.

Project 369: The Key to the Universe by David Kasneci—This book facilitates the creation of miracles.

Books on Abuse

Here is an expanded list of books on abuse for continued reading. These books offer valuable insights and perspectives on abuse, empowering readers to gain a deeper understanding of their experiences and find pathways to healing. Remember to choose the books that resonate with you and approach the content at your pace.

Empath and Narcissist by Lisa Kennedy: This book explores the dynamics between empaths and narcissists, offering guidance on navigating these relationships and establishing healthy boundaries.

Was It Even Abuse? by Emma Rose Byham: This book delves into the complexities of identifying and understanding abuse, helping readers gain clarity and validation for their experiences.

Power and Control by Sandra Horley: This book sheds light on the dynamics of power and control in abusive relationships, providing insights and strategies for breaking free from the cycle of abuse.

Why Does He Do That? by Lundy Bancroft: Written by a renowned expert in the field, this book examines the mindset and behaviors of abusive men, helping readers understand the underlying motivations and patterns of abuse.

The Sociopath Next Door by Martha Stout, PH.D.: This book explores the concept of sociopathy and its prevalence in society, offering insights into recognizing and protecting oneself from individuals with antisocial personality traits.

Healing from Hidden Abuse by Shannon Thomas, LCSW: This book explores the impact of covert and subtle forms of abuse, offering guidance on healing from these hidden traumas and reclaiming one's sense of self.

The Body Keeps the Score by Bessel van der Kolk, M.D.: This book explores the effects of trauma on the body and mind, offering a comprehensive understanding of the physiological and psychological impacts of abuse and providing strategies for healing.

Instagram Pages that I found incredibly helpful:

The following Instagram pages have been invaluable resources for me, providing information, inspiration, and a sense of community throughout my healing journey. I encourage you to explore their content and engage with the posts that resonate with your experiences. Remember, the goal is to glean insights that are beneficial to your unique path of healing and self-discovery.

@lisalu_girlpower: This Instagram page focuses on empowering individuals, particularly women, and provides inspiration and resources for personal growth and healing.

@the_enlightened_target: This page offers insights and awareness about narcissistic abuse, providing education and support for those who have experienced or are dealing with narcissistic individuals.

@understandingthenarc: This Instagram page aims to deepen understanding of narcissistic personality disorder and its effects, providing helpful information and resources for survivors of narcissistic abuse.

@healing_out.loud: This page promotes healing, self-care, and personal transformation, offering uplifting content and strategies for overcoming challenges and building resilience.

@shadowdeangelis: This Instagram page focuses on emotional healing and personal development, providing guidance and support for those recovering from toxic relationships and trauma.

@narcabusecoach: This Instagram page offers coaching and support for survivors of narcissistic abuse, providing tools and insights to aid in healing and reclaiming personal power.

@coachelizabethshaw: This Instagram page offers coaching, educational tools, and insights on NPD.

About the Author

Kia Lee is a graduate of The New School, where she earned her Bachelor of Fine Arts. Originally from Bucks County, Pennsylvania, she has spent the past two decades making New York City her home. Kia has a unique ability to share her vulnerabilities and challenges openly, creating a profound connection with her readers and fostering empathy and understanding. Her authentic voice and relatable writing style have resonated with many, as she passionately shares her personal journey with a global audience.

www.ingramcontent.com/pod-product-compliance
Ingram Content Group UK Ltd.
Pitfield, Milton Keynes, MK11 3LW, UK
UKHW062259290726
14090UKWH00017B/779